Brian Jackson:

Educational Innovator

Brian Jackson

Educational Innovator

Kit Hardwick

The Lutterworth Press

The Lutterworth Press
P.O. Box 60
Cambridge
CB1 2NT

www.lutterworth.com
publishing@lutterworth.com

ISBN 0 7188 3025 3

British Library Cataloguing in Publication Data
A catalogue record is available from the British Library

Printed in the United Kingdom by
MFP Print

Contents

Illustrations

Acknowledgements

I am indebted to the National Children's Centre, Huddersfield, with whose support this book has been published, and to its Director Hazel Wigmore.

I should also like to thank Mavis Woodward and Mark Kent, of the University of Huddersfield, who spent their six-weeks undergraduate work experience as research assistants to me at the National Children's Centre in 1994 and 1995 respectively. My thanks are due to Keith Laybourn, who, despite his Stakhanovite commitments, has read the manuscript and been an ever-available source of advice and support, and to Adrian Brink of The Lutterworth Press for his kind and helpful advice. Any errors that remain are entirely my responsibility.

In addition, I am hugely grateful for the time, patience, and kindness shown to me by all the people to whom I have written, telephoned, or who I have interviewed, during my researches. Their unfailing readiness to oblige me has been quite overwhelming. I believe this must, to a considerable extent, reflect the cordiality of their memories of my subject: Brian Jackson.

Preface

Brian Jackson, whose short life was packed with both successful and unsuccessful schemes to help his fellow men, is sadly now almost forgotten. A book on the varied career of Michael Young, who described Brian as 'talented and a good organiser' and 'the most outstanding of the colleagues I have had', and who according to Michael, originally prompted the idea of an open university, mentions him only twice in footnotes as co-writer of two articles.[1] After an early career full of brilliance and promise Brian Jackson died tragically young, unemployed, and possibly unemployable, drinking heavily and given to bouts of depression, though still capable of scintillating on his visits to the media and to his beloved Huddersfield.[2] The purpose of this book is to argue for the importance of his influence in helping to change society and to explain his sad later decline.

Brian Jackson was one of that new group of post-Butler boys – girls did not figure prominently – who won scholarships from working-class homes, went to grammar schools and in many cases on to university. They came out into the world slightly fazed, having amassed a new set of middle-class ideas and social mores, yet frequently feeling a nostalgia bordering on guilt for the culture they had left behind. Richard Hoggart from an earlier generation, later a friend of Brian's, was the first to try to resolve this dilemma in *The Uses of Literacy* and Raymond Williams's *Culture and Society* is widely regarded as the definitive example of this *genre*. Brian himself wrote a book on the subject *Working Class Community* which, though not pub-lished until 1968 actually began life ten years previously. In the introduction Brian wrote, 'My chief debt in preparing this book is to Dennis Marsden who did so much of the early fieldwork and writing up.'[3] Dennis Marsden was working for the Institute of Community Studies 'in a lowly capacity as an interviewer,' as a result of Brian's encouragement.[4] Brian and he proposed to Michael Young, the director of the Institute, that they should research a book on working-class communities and it was only later that Michael suggested that they change their focus and do a book on grammar schools, which of course they did.[5] Brian described their motivation as follows,

> The study began in 1958, out of that debate on working-class life that blazed up, and died down, so very quickly. *The Uses of Literacy* was fresh on the bookstalls, so was *Saturday Night and Sunday*

Morning. On television Dennis Mitchell was showing *Morning in the Streets*. The papers were attending to the work on family and kinship that Michael Young and his colleagues were reporting from Bethnal Green. And the whole structure of our school and university system was clarified by findings of untapped working-class talent recorded in such surveys as Floud, Halsey and Martin's *Social Class and Educational Opportunity*. Looking back, we can see that there was an element of fashion in the extent to which this debate was taken up.[6]

Chas Critcher explains this sudden interest in working-class communities thus,

There *were* important changes in the nature of British society in the post-war period. . . . It is only an apparent paradox that the serious study of working-class culture should emerge just at that moment when it was being loudly proclaimed that the working class had ceased to exist. The discovery of working-class culture was a *response* to this argument.[7]

Brian Jackson outlined the elements of this study in three stages. First *Family and Kinship* looked at the strengths of working-class family ties centred on a strong matriarch, but as he points out, such an interpretation was challenged by Madeleine Kerr's picture of a Liverpool 'problem family' *Ship Street*, where he noted, the 'restrictive and smothering role of Mum, whose emotional hold makes it difficult for the children ever to break away.[8] In the same vein was Dennis, Henriques and Slaughter's *Coal is Our Life* which showed the

Mutual help and personal generosities between the men, but also suggested that the women's life especially was one of subjection (contraceptives thrown on the fire because they took all the enjoyment out of sex, husband's wages never known, violence at night when he returned with a skinful of ale).[9]

The second strand dealt with education and social welfare while a third line of enquiry, according to Brian, 'concerned itself with the nature and effect of the mass media.'

Probably the most important achievement here of writers such as Richard Hoggart and Raymond Williams has been to break up the easy concept of working-class 'masses' being given the rubbish they ask for and being well satisfied with it.[10]

Brian then cited Williams's dictum, 'Masses are other people. There are in fact no masses; there are only ways of seeing people as masses.' Although this is his only reference to Williams it is important as an insight into the way Brian wanted to base his research. Critcher quotes from Willams' conclusion to *Culture and Society*

The primary distinction between bourgeois and working class [sic]

culture is to be sought in the whole way of life, and here, again, we must not confine ourselves to such evidence as housing, dress and modes of leisure. Industrial production tends to create uniformity in such matters, but the vital distinction lies at a different level. The crucial distinguishing element in English life since the Industrial Revolution is not language, not dress, not leisure. . . . The crucial distinction is between alternative ideas of the nature of social relationship.[11]

This is precisely what *Working Class Community* seeks to illuminate. Brian describes his method as 'listening to the voices'.[12] He goes on to dismiss John Braine, Arnold Wesker, Alan Sillitoe whose versions of working class life have 'never strongly moved' him. They are, according to Brian,

Too close to the sociologist or the documentary reporter to offer the kind of creative experience I'm concerned with here. That, I think, can be found with authority in three artists from the industrial north – the painter L.S. Lowry, the novelist D. H. Lawrence, and the sculptor Henry Moore.[13]

Brian would doubtless, therefore, have been proud of the accolade he received from Keith Waterhouse in the *Sunday Times* which is quoted on the back cover of the *Penguin* edition of *Working Class Community*, 'He brings the novelist's as well as the sociologist's eye to his subject.'

Certainly Brian seems to have been in a trap between the disciplines of literature and sociology and between some vague sense of a warm and supportive community whose values were somehow threatened by mass-media culture on the one hand and, for those like himself who had been through it, by higher education and the 'high' culture of Matthew Arnold on the other. He never seems to have totally resolved this dichotomy in his own case. Indeed, he is the archetypal problem adult of the peer group which he and Dennis Marsden studied in *Education and the Working Class*.

But Brian's generation of young and talented people, having grown up during wartime and post-war austerity, burst onto the scene in the 1950s as 'Angry Young Men' and 'Ban-the-Bomb-ers' and set the scene for the swinging, 'can-do', sixties which began with the trial of *Lady Chatterley's Lover* and ended soon after the oil crisis of 1973. Brian was very much a part of that movement and, shunning a formal academic career, launched himself into a myriad schemes to help the under-privileged: the poor, the young, the old, and immigrants, not to mention his work for people abroad.

In his brief lifetime he worked especially in the field of education. He was concerned with those who had missed out, which led to his creating, almost single-handedly, the National Extension College, NEC, in 1963, as a model for the Open University. In the 1970s he worked hard to promote childminding as a cost-effective alternative to nursery education for all; a seemingly still-too-expensive goal for society to achieve. Towards the end of his life he was promoting schemes for the on-going education of the new young-retired leisure class.

Michael Sanderson has written that it was Brian Jackson's book *Streaming* which led to unease about the 11-plus exam as it showed that children were being selected as early as seven or eight into fast or slow streams in preparation for the exam.[14] Brian Simon, himself among the leading campaigners for the abolition of streaming in junior schools, wrote that *Streaming*, demonstrated the 'almost complete hegemony of streaming in the early 1960s dramatically and convincingly'.[15] Moreover he regards Brian Jackson's confirmation of the relation, 'long suspected', between streaming and social class as most significant and, commenting on the book's date of publication, 1964, says that the Plowden Committee was then beginning to realise that this was *the* crucial issue in the reconstruction of the primary school. Finally Simon comments that within 'a mere fifteen years' of the book's publication streaming had almost totally disappeared.[16]

Most important perhaps, as Director of the Advisory Centre for Education (ACE) during the 1960s, Brian campaigned for comprehensive education and greater parental involvement in schools as well as trying to find ways to use the public schools more democratically. He was perhaps the most ardent opponent of those who, led by Eric James and Harry Ree (the latter subsequently came to agree with Brian), championed excellence rather than equality. Brian Jackson, through his personal charisma and his media skills, had a considerable influence on social change in his lifetime.

Two decades after Brian's death, education and the welfare of young people are still among the most immediate concerns of government. Brian's life and work are surely relevant today: virtually all the topics in which Brian Jackson was involved are subjects that are still very much in the forefront of debate under the present administration.

Notes

1. Dench Geoff, Tony Flower, and Kate Gavron, eds. *Young at Eighty*, pp.226, 227, Transcript, Michael Young interviewed by Paul Thompson. National Sound Archive, Letter, Michael Young to Sonia Jackson, 4 July 1983. See Chapter 3.
2. Interviews with Neville Butler, 3 May 1996, Godfrey Smith, 26 April 1997, and John Cashman, 20 May 1997. Hazel Wigmore would prefer this sentence to have been omitted or at least to have read . . .'tragically young with no salaried employment and no new research contracts offered . . . as always drinking heavily. . .'.
3. Brian Jackson, *Working Class Community*, p.vii.
4. Letter from Dennis Marsden, 12 December 1997.
5. *idem.*
6. Brian Jackson, *Working Class Community*, p4.
7. Chas Critcher, 'Sociology, cultural studies and the post-war working class,' in John Clarke, Chas Critcher and Richard Johnson, *Working-Class Culture.*
8. Brian Jackson, *Working Class Community*, pp.4-5.

9. *ibid.* p.6.

10. *ibid.* p.8.

11. Chas Critcher, *Working Class Culture*, p.37.

12. Brian Jackson, *Working Class Community*, p.3.

13. *idem.*

14. Michael Sanderson, *Educational Opportunity*, p.50

15. Brian Simon, *Education and the Social Order 1940-1990*, pp346-350.

16. *ibid.* p.370.

Chapter 1
Early days

Brian Jackson was born 28 December 1932 at Kirks Place, a small back-to-back house set in a square in Huddersfield in what was then the West Riding of Yorkshire.[1] At the age of five, although the family was Roman Catholic, Brian went to the local Moldgreen council school, as, in due course, did his younger siblings Derek and Maureen.[2] Both his cousin Dolly and his sister Maureen remember him being bookish from an early age and according to Maureen he had a drawerful of *Everyman* classics while still at Moldgreen. Yet school itself seems to have bored him. Although he was to campaign vigorously as an adult against streaming he was driven by his junior school to absent himself.

> I was an episodic truant myself all through school, with long yawning stretches between six and nine years old. All I remember is how difficult it was to fill out the fugitive hours from corn flakes-time till the school bell let the gang out. Catching green flies in the park, breaking into lean-to allotment greenhouses, sitting with old men on the warm pipes along the indoor Market, and visits to the lavatory like punctuation marks in a problematic day.[3]

Nevertheless at eleven he passed the exam for the prestigious local single-sex grammar school, Huddersfield College, despite suffering from a severe attack of scarlet fever. This illness which in those pre-antibiotic days was treated in an isolation hospital prevented him from sitting the second part of the examination but he appears to have written such an outstanding first paper that the authorities accepted him on that basis alone.[4] It may have been this infection, too, that caused him to wear the pebbly and unflattering national-health glasses that his later colleague, Dennis Marsden, remembers as a part of Brian's generally unprepossessing youthful appearance.[5] He never wore glasses as an adult.

In 1948 Brian went into the Lower VI Arts four months before his sixteenth birthday. He took English, French and History coming top in English and History at the end of his first term. His form master commented favourably and added that Brian was prominent in the Debating Society.[6] In due course he was accepted at St Catharine's College, Cambridge, to read English. The story of how he got to Cambridge is that he only heard of the place from a fellow pupil, thought it sounded nice, and wrote off. This sounds like one of Brian's leg-pulls. Dennis Marsden wrote that 'Oxford and Cambridge were what that school was about', and described how in assembly he read daily on the honours board the achievements of previous (Oxbridge) scholarship

Brian (centre) with Derek and Maureen.

winners.[7] Another version appears in a review Brian wrote of two books about Oxford and Cambridge by former students.[8] At all events there is a consensus on the outcome. Having torn up his headmaster's reference which he had opened and read he calmly told his interviewer that it had not done him justice. The dons apparently agreed and he was accepted.

Brian also made his presence felt among his contemporaries through the sheer force of his personality and strength of his opinions. 'If Brian said so-and-so was so, he bloody well meant it.' according to Malcolm Kaye, a friend from the Huddersfield Jazz Club, whose brother Trevor christened Brian 'The Master' as a result. The name was taken up by Harold Mettrick (Henry Dibb) and Dennis Marsden.[9] Though they used it sarcastically, according to Malcolm it concealed an underlying admission of his intellectual leadership of the group.[10] It was this self-confidence and total conviction of the rightness of his own views, doubtless reinforced by his subsequent intellectual achievements at Cambridge, that became one of Brian's greatest strengths. Yet it also produced an intolerance in him that could be irritating and may well later have proved an obstacle to his ability to adapt to a changing world.

Brian described the Jazz Club some years later in a chapter in *Working Class Community* as a peripatetic affair; a moveable feast alighting for a while in a room in a pub or club before moving on to fresh pastures at the whim of its members or the landlord of the premises, sometimes dividing to multiply, amoeba-like, into a break-away group, only to regroup when tempers cooled. He also as Alan Sinfield remarks felt that the ethos of the club was a refreshing alternative to the stultifying conventionality of the school and that it was, for him, a glimpse of a broader world of culture: 'If the life of New Orleans was an exaggerated image of working-class life, the stimulating generalised emotions of jazz were a hazy image of what the world of art could offer.'[11]

It was through the Jazz Club that Brian met Sheila Mannion who was to become his first wife. Sheila was sixteen and ravishingly pretty, always well-dressed and much in demand at parties.[12] Brian at twenty and fresh back from national service in the desert was captivated. Brian went up to Cambridge that autumn where he joined his two former school friends, also members of the Jazz Club set back home; Dennis Marsden, who was then an engineer, and Hal Mettrick, a mathematician and would-be blues singer, who were both already up since neither had elected to do his national service before going to university. Hal Mettrick remembers Brian's arrival being 'like a breath of fresh air' and both he and Dennis Marsden were fired by Brian's enthusiasm for literature and especially poetry.[13] Brian was already showing the first signs of that power to inspire and motivate others that was to be a feature of his subsequent life. Very soon another of his life-long traits, his manipulation of the Press, was to make its first appearance. At the end of his first year all three went on an expedition, organised by Danish students, to search for gold above the Arctic Circle in Lapland.[14] Brian's plan was that the three should pay for the trip by writing about it and to this end he divided the major newspapers between them. Although they earned a small amount in this way they took holiday jobs as bus conductors or labourers in Hudders-field to earn most of the money – the £50 – they needed.[15] But clearly Brian, who had placed his story with the *Daily Express*, had realised that the papers were always hungry for copy and could thus be used for free publicity.

Dennis Marsden had been very unhappy during his time at Cambridge, as he bravely recalled in a brief autobiographical note, failing to fulfil the social aspirations his overly ambitious parents had for him whilst hating himself for conniving at their snobbishness. He also found himself academically to be a square peg in a round hole; having elected to specialise in science in the sixth form because it was in those days the most fashionable subject, he found it both hard work and boring at university.[16] After completing his national service he applied, at Brian's suggestion, to the Institute of Community Studies, newly set up by Michael Young. The Institute had just 'won the pools' to use Dennis's phrase. The Joseph Rowntree Trust, which was originally set up to fund workers' housing projects like New Earswick near York, had found itself superfluous when both major political parties enthusiastically espoused building council houses after the war, and in consequence had just changed its rules so as to be able to fund a broader spectrum of social welfare. As a result, it had allotted the institute £75,000. Dennis was taken on and sent to Toynbee Hall (the social settlement in East London named after the Victorian social reformer Arnold Toynbee) for a spell, to learn something of interviewing techniques.[17]

The social anomie experienced by Dennis Marsden may not have been unique to the 1950s but it was certainly and overtly prevalent then. It may have been partly a result of more working-class children, mostly boys, going through grammar school and on to university after Butler's Education Act of 1944, or possibly was just part of the social upheaval of the war itself where,

Brian (centre), on National Service, with native servant?

through things like evacuation and rationing people saw, for the first time, how the other half of society lived. It was evoked most brilliantly in 1954 by Kingsley Amis, whose epony-mous hero, 'Lucky Jim' Dixon, though clearly middle class by edu-cation was like a fish out of water in the social milieu of his awful professor, Welch. Embarrassed by his gaucheness yet at the same time perceptive enough to see through their pretensions, he resolved his dilemma by running away with the prettiest girl of their set.[18] This tendency for male hypergamy, while not new, was prevalent enough in the 1950s for it to be the subject of pieces of fiction such as *Room at the Top* and *Look Back In Anger*, while anthropologist Geoffrey Gorer devoted a whole essay to the phenomenon.[19]

After university Brian taught for some years in local primary schools at Whittlesford and Cambridge. It was this experience, no doubt, that first opened his eyes to how much less successful some children already were by the age of five at absorbing new information if they had not previously been stimulated by creative play. He found that children with articulate parents who talked to them and tried to answer all their questions had a huge advantage already before they started formal education. In short, the middle-class child was ahead in the education race right from the cradle. Streaming – then almost universally practised in larger primary schools anxious to maximise their eleven-plus success rate – only served to emphasise the differential. It seemed to Brian that this was not in the spirit of Lord Butler's 1944 Act.

Perhaps Brian's thoughts were already turning towards the idea of sociology in preference to education as a career for himself. His book *Streaming* based on his teaching experience illustrates graphically the problems facing the working-class child. At the time, in 1958, Richard Hoggart's classic social commentary on northern working-class life, *The Uses of Literacy*, was published. This made a huge impression on Brian. Richard Hoggart has written, and Sheila Abrams confirmed, how Brian went to introduce himself to Hoggart and declared that they were to become friends, which indeed they did.[20] This ability to approach famous people who were complete strangers and to be accepted by them was another of

Brian's talents that manifested itself early on. Sheila and Dennis both remember Brian taking them to see 'Mr' Lowry. Brian not only bought two pictures on 'tick' – none of them had any cash at the time – but so admired another small picture that the artist made him a present of it.[21]

Brian, settling down to teaching in Cambridge, did not seem to be as socially displaced as Dennis. But he too seems to have felt another sort of anomie. He thought that they had burned their boats almost from the day they started at grammar school. There was no going back to their roots. He wrote how, from the start, he played with other grammar school boys and *not* with the neighbours' children and how he moved in the world of 'the home and the womenfolk', while 'The world of the men, and their sons who were to succeed them (in the factory or mill) we never saw, or even contemplated.'[22] In the introduction to the paperback edition of *Education and the Working Class* he wrote '. . . the voices [of their interviewees] weave their own pattern of delight, snobbery, frustration and love' and the last of a series of quotations illustrating those themes could have come straight from the lips of himself or Dennis 'I like to go back and I still like visiting. I like to go round and hear relations talking about themselves . . . but I'm not sure, . . . I'm not sure whether it's quite the same interest as I used to have, or if I regard them more as . . . well . . . specimens.'[23]

Brian Jackson's socialism seems to have been inspired originally by having felt himself treated as a second-class citizen at school, and sparked into active flame by Richard Hoggart's *The Uses of Literacy*. His brand of socialism together with his passion for literature would surely explain his lifelong struggle to resolve the dichotomy between his reverence for a rather romanticised working-class culture, and his desire to bring the 'sweetness and light' of 'the central culture of our society' to the masses.[24]

Whatever the motivation, Brian decided he wanted to add his pennyworth to the increasingly fashionable field of 'community studies' and in his direct way, as Michael Young later wrote, he introduced himself and announced this to be his intention. 'Can you write?' said Young. 'Of course' was Brian's reply.[25] The result was *Education and the Working Class* which was published as a report of the Institute of Community Studies by Routledge and Kegan Paul, on 2 February 1962, at twenty-eight shillings (£1.40).

Brian, Dennis Marsden and Sheila Jackson, as she then was, carried out a pilot study of a working-class community, a subject which they knew intimately and which, at the same time, was clearly a splendidly topical subject in those days of massive slum clearances where whole communities were being uprooted and moved into new tower blocks surrounded by open spaces, lawns, and trees. They looked at the world of northern working-men's clubs as manifested in Huddersfield: a world of brass bands, allotments, and pigeon racing. But also, as they saw it, a world where dour individualism and non-conformity combined with co-operation and self-help. It was a man's world where beer was cheap, humour could be crude, and women were only present at weekends by invitation. They received a small grant from the Frederick Soddy Trust for this investigation and, as a result of their report, Brian secured funding from the Joseph Rowntree Memorial Trust's grant to the Institute of Community Studies to enable him to join Dennis full time as a researcher. Their subject, prompted by Michael Young as previously noted, was themselves. That is to say, they decided to look at a group of their contemporaries who, like them, had gone from working-class homes to grammar school and thence to higher education at university or teacher-training college. They celebrated their decision, as Dennis Marsden told me, 'in a typically working-class way by having halibut for tea'.[26]

The methodology was straightforward but would be unthinkable in today's Data-Protection-Act climate of sensitivity about access to personal information stored on computers. They simply went to the offices of their former school, Huddersfield College, and of the other three grammar schools in Huddersfield, and got the secretary to let them examine the pass lists of the Higher School Certificate and G.C.E. 'A'-level examinations which they checked against details of parents' occupations, also provided by the school records. They selected the years between 1949 and 1952 so that the men and women would then be in their mid- and late-twenties, as they felt it important to talk to adults who might already have become parents themselves. This method produced 49 boys but only about half that number of girls and they had to extend the period of the sample for girls to redress this imbalance. Eventually they had a group of 88 former working-class children. They obtained their addresses and proceeded to follow them up and interview them. In addition, taking note of other recent researches in a similar field, they interviewed all the parents separately so as to glean as much information as possible on the 'home background'.[27]

At the suggestion of Michael Young they also reported briefly on a 'control' group of ten randomly picked middle-class students from the same schools,[28] providing a rationale for the whole study by posing two questions: why, proportionately to their numbers in society, do so many middle-class children successfully complete the total grammar school course and go on to university? Conversely, why is it that relatively few working-class children do so? They concluded that middle-class parents had a 'shrewd and trusting understanding' with the schools and teachers and that 'in a host of small but telling ways', they had been able to use the state system to advantage their offspring or sustain them through bad patches, 'even against the schools' opinion' at times. The resulting adults were often close to their parents, though with apparently slightly more sensitised and widely cultured outlooks, who perpetuated their parents' spirit of self-help in vigorous pursuit of mostly professional careers.

The successful working-class children also appeared mainly to come from homes where ambition and respectability, often going hand in hand with church or chapel membership, or active participation in some other social organisation such as trade-union or friendly society, were of paramount importance. Such families, 'sunken-middle' class rather than merely prosperous working class, often had access through relatives or social contacts to some of the sorts of information which helped the middle classes to advantage their children. These tended to be families with only one or two children and they often lived in areas where the local school served a largely middle-class population. The respectability could often spill over into snobbishness – an un-neighbourliness uncharacteristic of northern working-class society as a whole and commonly thought to be 'stand-offish' – while the ambition often led to the children feeling under great pressure to succeed. These insights, reflecting their own experiences, found a ready response in generations of undergraduates and trainee teachers. Kate Soar, a Cambridge friend of Brian's who came from a similar background, with her Lancastrian bluntness put it thus: 'We thought we were rather clever until we read Brian's book. Then we realised we just all had pushy mothers'.

It was not just having pushy mothers, however, that led to success. As Brian had already found as a result of his primary-school teaching, an early ability to read led to selection at an early age for placement in the fast or 'A' stream where children who looked to have academic promise were specially nurtured: of course the result of this practice was a self-fulfilling prophecy. This process continued at the grammar school where, combined with the 'strangeness and sheer difference' of the place in some cases it led to a feeling of alienation and inferiority especially for those plunged back into 'B' or 'C' streams. Some children also suffered from a loss of social life, cut off from their neighbourhood, and a few rebelled; preferring, for example, to play for the youth club rather than the school team. Several, exposed for the first time to middle-class assumptions, attitudes, and even accents, reported feeling bewildered by the whole experience. But many working-class children, anxious to please ambitious parents, or in some cases in order to subsume their feelings of social inferiority, threw themselves into the life and especially the work of the grammar school with a vengeance. These children learned to conform. They consciously changed their accents – though often keeping a local patois for home use – and they pursued academic excellence in fierce competition with each other. Some admitted to having few friends: they had rivals instead. Many of them, as the rebels left at sixteen, went into the sixth form and became prefects. By this stage a disproportionate number of them were scaling the heights: fourteen became head or deputy-head boy or girl and a quarter of them got to Oxbridge.

There was a downside to this. Many of the sample achieved only mediocre degrees: one at least, Brian's close friend Hal Mettrick, (Henry Dibb) having previously won an Open Scholarship. Brian's major concern, however, and one which preoccupied him for the rest of his life, was that in succeeding academically these people had assumed a middle-class culture and had shed, like an old coat, all vestiges of the warmth and humanity that he saw in

Four Dudes: from left, Dennis Marsden, Hal Mettrick,
Malcolm Kaye and Brian Jackson.

northern working-class society. Most, in Brian's view, were little more than self-satisfied conformists, expressing hostility to comprehensive education, yet feeling inferior to people who had been to public schools – they made friends with 'an American or a Persian student' more easily than with a 'fellow Yorkshireman from Giggleswick' – and some of them had turned into insufferable prigs.[29] Over half of them and in the case of the girls three-quarters had become teachers, often by default or in order to remain in an environment where they had achieved success. It is easy to see how depressing these findings were for the authors.

There were three main themes illustrated by the investigation. The first, that despite the 1944 Butler Education Act which removed fees from secondary education, there were virtually no more working-class children benefiting from the system by completing a successful sixth-form education than before, was not new. As the authors reported, both Floud, Halsey, and Martin's *Social Class and Educational Opportunity*, published by Heinemann in 1957, and the 1959 Crowther Report *15 to 18* had made this clear, and they had taken this as their starting point. Secondly they showed that possibly the main reason for this was the appalling lack of information available to working-class parents and children about what was possible, both in terms of career structure and of financial assistance for higher education. They recognised too that for many working-class families the economic constraints necessitated their children leaving school and starting work long before the question of university grants arose. And thirdly they showed in their interviews with the young adults how conclusively they had rejected virtually all that their parents had stood for. That section of the book ends with a reference to a Jack London novel where a midshipman is urged not to abjure the lower decks when he reaches the high places:

> Today most of these 88 children have developed into stable, often rigidly orthodox citizens, . . . [who] now find themselves much nearer the 'high places'. But it would be sentimental to report that the majority of them, though discharging their duties to parents, wanted (in any testing way] to 'remember'. Most wish to forget.[30]

Inevitably, it seems, these findings helped shape Brian's future career as an agitator for educational reform. Together with his own experience, the research would seem to have convinced him of the need to disseminate information about educational possibilities much more widely, especially to the working class. This was to occupy much of the next ten years of his life. It appears more than likely that these ideas must have filtered through to Michael Young long before publication and that they influenced his decision in 1960 to set up the Advisory Centre for Education which, with its magazine *Where?* was intended to meet this need. Publication of the book confirmed Dennis Marsden in his move from chemical engineering, which he had studied at Cambridge, to social science, which went on to teach at the University of Essex. But, if the book influenced the lives of the writers, what influence did it have on our society at large?

A sociologist has written, 'I know of no better sociological account of the personal costs of class mobility'.[31] A former editor of *New Society* has said it was one of the books which helped to popularise sociology and thereby help create a market for his journal.[32] Sales of the book would seem to justify these assessments. The revised edition of *Education and the Working Class* was first published in paperback in June 1966 and sold 14,400 copies in the rest of that year.[33] The following year Routledge, whose stocks were down to 240 copies of the hardback were none too pleased at having to re-set the whole book for a fourth impression as the paperback named the fictional 'Marburton' as Huddersfield which does not have the same number of letters.[34] The paperback has been reprinted several times and it continued to sell in tens of thousands of copies in subsequent years, topping the hundred thousand mark by 1973. It regularly sold several hundred copies a year in Australia. The book has been, and remains, on student reading lists – where it is frequently described as the most enjoyable title on the list – ever since it was first published, and its readership by now must be well over a million.[35]

In confirming previous findings about how the education system was failing to process all suitable candidates for higher education – Crowther had shown nearly half the boys entering National Service with an I.Q. of 120-plus had left school at sixteen – it illuminated the failures and iniquities of the selection, or streaming, process and showed beyond doubt how it favoured the middle-class child. In part two of the book the authors press the case for comprehensive education and its wide readership, aided no doubt by its readability, must have played a part in changing the climate of opinion especially amongst the more articulate section of the labour-voting community. The historian of education, Brian Simon, notes that although the Labour Party had endorsed the idea of 'multilateral' schools as early as 1939, neither Ellen Wilkinson nor George Tomlinson, the two Ministers of Education in Labour's post-war administrations, attempted to implement such a policy.[36] Many of Labour's leaders had, like the authors, been to grammar schools themselves. Although Harold Wilson, the Labour leader, declared that the grammar schools would be abolished 'over [his] dead body' the principle of comprehensive education became official party policy with the issue of Anthony Crosland's Circular 10/65 (12 July 1965) which requested Local Education Authorities to make comprehensive schools the normal pattern within five years. Brian's obituary notice in *The Times Educational Supplement* described *Education and the Working Class as* 'a powerful lever in the campaign for comprehensives'.[37]

Having analysed the problems of the grammar schools for working-class children and looked at the loss of all that they considered worthwhile in working-class culture as a result of traditional higher education, the book concludes with a positive note. The authors proposed a solution. This would entail a university with 'a large new working-class intake. One reaction to this', they admitted, 'may be the 'more will be worse' cry: extending university education will lower the general standard in an impossible way. Perhaps it needs to be said that this is not what has happened in previous expansions in other countries.' Furthermore this new institution, they proposed, should be a university which 'involves itself in local life, rather than dominates or defies it from behind college or red-brick walls.' They called this the 'open' university.[38] It was, so far as anyone can remember, the first time ever that this phrase was used.

Brian Jackson and Dennis Marsden's book was to be an influence not just on those generations of working-class children who passed through grammar schools and saw themselves, and their contemporaries, in its pages. It also helped to persuade a wider readership to believe that comprehensive education was preferable to the system that then existed. Not least it influenced the lives of its authors as in their different ways they shifted into new careers. Brian Jackson was never to go back to school teaching, as shortly after the publication of the book he was invited by Michael Young to become director of his new, but foundering, Advisory Centre for Education, ACE. Brian's rescue and development of that organisation forms the substance of the next chapter.

Notes

1. Interview with Brian Jackson's sister, Maureen Jones, 17 May 1994.
2. Brian, in later life, rejoiced at his mother's decision not to send him to the Roman Catholic school. Interview with Sonia Jackson, 17 August 1993.
3. Brian Jackson 'Truancy-A Pilot Study', MS, September 1974, F1.
4. Interview with Maureen Jones, 17 May 1994.
5. Interview with Dennis Marsden, 21 September 1994.
6. School report, SJ1.
7. Dennis Marsden in Ronald Goldman, ed., *Breakthrough*, p.117.
8. 'Secrets, style and ritual.' *Guardian*, 31 March 1977.
9. Hal Mettrick features as Henry Dibb in *Education and the Working Class*.
10. Interview with Malcolm Kaye, 31 October 1994.
11. Alan Sinfield, *Postwar Britain*, p.160.
12. Several interviewees and the writer, who met Mrs Abrams in September 1994, attest to her looks.
13. Interview with Hal Mettrick, 30 December 1994.
14. 'Adventure Boys Seek Lapland Gold', *Daily Express*, 5 July 1954. SJ2.
15. *Daily Express, idem*, Interview with Hal Mettrick, 30 December 1994.
16. Dennis Marsden in B*reakthrough.*
17. Interview with Dennis Marsden, 21 September 1994.
18. Kingsley Amis, *Lucky Jim.*
19. Geoffrey Gorer, 'The Perils of Hypergamy', in Feldman, G., and M. Gartenberg, eds. *Protest: The Beat Generation and the Angry Young Men*, pp. 315-319.
20. Richard Hoggart, 'The inventive idealist from the West Riding', *Sunday Times* 11 July 1993, p. 65. Interview with Sheila Abrams, 21 September 1994.
21. Interviews with Sheila Abrams, *idem*, Dennis Marsden, 21 September 1994, and Hal Mettrick, 30 December 1994.
22. Brian Jackson, autobiographical notes in *Working Men's Clubs in Huddersfield – A Preliminary Enquiry*, Brian Jackson, Dennis Marsden, and Sheila Jackson, 1958, C2.
23. Brian Jackson and Dennis Marsden, *Education and the Working Class,* p16. Unless otherwise stated all future references will be to this revised edition.
24. *Ibid.*, p.243.
25. Michael Young 'A tribute to Brian Jackson', *Where?*, September 1983 p.3.
26. Interview with Dennis Marsden, 21 September 1994.
27. *Idem*, plus Jackson and Marsden, *Education and the Working Class* pp.58, 217.
28. Interview with Dennis Marsden, 21 September 1994.
29. Jackson and Marsden, *Education and the Working Class*, p.166.
30. Jackson and Marsden, *Education and the Working Class*, p.214.
31. Gordon Marshall, *In Praise of Sociology*, p.5.
32. Interview with Paul Barker, 6 June 1997.
33. Letter from Jonathon Croall, Penguin, to Brian Jackson, 23 July 1973, C4.
34. Letter from Norman Franklin, Routledge, to Brian Jackson, 22 May 1967, C4.
35. Several people in casual conversation with the author during his researches confirm this view of the book.
36. Brian Simon, *The State and Educational Change*, pp.165-167.
37. 'Epitaph for a man of ideas', *The Times Educational Supplement, 8* July 1983.
38. Jackson and Marsden, *Education and the Working Class*, p.246.

Chapter 2
The Advisory Centre for Education:
the first ten years

The 1960s were to be Brian Jackson's decade. He single-handedly built the Advisory Centre for Education, ACE into a major organisation through his ability to convince people that things *could* be made to happen, and that *they* could play a significant part. He manipulated the media and, though ACE ultimately failed in its aim of bringing information to the working classes, there were many successes among the causes for which it campaigned. Still of relevance today, these included greater parental involvement in schools, the universities' clearing house scheme, and the restructuring of primary education following the Plowden report. The purpose of this chapter is to show how Brian Jackson's flair, energy and, above all commitment to his belief in a fairer society enabled him to motivate others and to build ACE into a formidable force for educational reform.

ACE was started in Bethnal Green in 1960 under the aegis of Michael Young. It was conceived as an educational version of the Consumers' Association, which Young had also helped to set up, and its main aim was to produce a magazine for the consumers of education similar to *Which?* the publication which tested and reported on products and services for the general public. It is a voluntary body, registered as an educational charity and is governed by an Independent Council. Such prominent writers on educational matters as John Vaizey and Tyrrell Burgess had been associated with it briefly but when Young moved to Cambridge in 1962 it was, in his own words, 'so much in the doldrums that it looked as though it could not be revived'.[1] Indeed, the Autumn issue of 1961 had been reduced to the pedestrian level of giving profiles of all the Ministry of Education staff; hardly headline material.

During the next dozen years Brian Jackson built ACE into a self-financing centre of information on educational matters, disseminated, together with its radical proposals for reform, through its own house magazine *Where?* and through a hugely successful campaign of self-publicity in the national press.

Brian, according to Michael Young, agreed to try to rescue the project and became its new director. With almost no funding to begin with he rented a single room in Bateman Street, Cambridge, for £1 a week, and began to gather round him volunteers. One of the first of these was Young's wife, Sasha, who became Editor of *Where?*, the magazine that was to be to education what *Which?* was to commerce and industry. Sonia Abrams, who later became Sonia Jackson, was another early recruit who joined the team that summer as the Secretary and subsequently held several key positions including the editorship of *Where?* The couple met when Brian, returning by train to Cambridge after a BBC interview, met Philip Abrams who invited him home to supper. The treasurer, Howard Dickinson, and Young himself as Chairman were the only two to survive from the original ACE group. Brian's association with Michael Young had begun in 1958 when he approached Young's Institute of Community Studies for help and advice. In a project written by a student-teacher on Brian's work at ACE Brian is described, presumably by himself, as one of the 'movers' in the founding of ACE.[2] But he was clearly the person who *really* created ACE. In the words of one director of a funding charity who knew both men well it was Brian who, 'always an exciting and charismatic figure' was 'capable, with his energy, vigour and flair, of turning Michael Young's ideas, which were not always practicable, into something which could be developed'.[3] The two men were, in John Henniker's words, 'an ideal and unique combination'.

This assessment is borne out by Young's memory of the office in the early days of Brian's tenure at ACE as one of the busiest rooms he had ever known, and his view that it was Brian's 'energy, flair, capacity to inspire confidence in his volunteers,' together with his gift for 'brilliant description' that made the whole thing work.[4] Brian seems to have put his new-found prominence as an author to immediate good use writing 'A Place for Parents in Education' and 'Streaming in Junior Schools' for the *Guardian* on 29 and 30 June 1962. Both were themes he was to pursue vigorously for many years.

Indeed, Brian's first priority at ACE was to encourage and facilitate choice for parents and students. Immediately there is a conundrum, as so often there is with the causes Brian promoted, in that the ultimate choice in education is only available to the very wealthy: the option of sending one's child to a public school. And despite his egalitarianism – he proposed that Princess Anne should be sent to a comprehensive school – Brian acknowledged that independent schools could have a useful role to play, if only as working laboratories for educational experiment. A.S. Neill's Summerhill was Brian's preferred example for this type of work.[5]

Yet within the state system choice often meant that the better-educated parents chose the best schools for their children which led to *more* not less inequality. And zoning, theoretically creating neighbourhood schools, in practice frequently meant rationing of the more favoured schools. The only choice available to most parents and children eventually came down to a choice *within* one school. Parents could influence such matters as the subjects their children studied, religious education, the school's policy on rewards and punishments and whether they would leave their children's education entirely in the hands of the teachers or take an active interest themselves. Even this was, in those days, widely discouraged. One of Brian's first acts was to photograph and publicise a school notice board prohibiting parents from the playground and setting strict limits on visiting or meeting the staff.[6] He heartily disapproved of this 'Keep Out, Trespassers Will Be Prosecuted' attitude adopted in those days by many head teachers.

Another problem Brian encountered in the early days was the lack of informative literature for parents and with few exceptions of anyone capable of producing it. There were journalists who could write but knew nothing about education on the one hand, and educationalists who knew the facts but wrote stuffy and jargon-filled texts on the other. *Where?* not only became a central reference store of educational information unique to the United Kingdom – no other country had anything like it – but it also pitched a level and a style for the dialogue between the system and those who used it.[7]

Research into education in those days was limited too. Much of it was concerned with specialised psychological enquiry or with questions of measurement, testing and evaluation, largely centred on the eleven-plus examinations. But *Where?* provided a platform for an informal layman's discussion of the work of such as A.H. Halsey and Jean Floud, and subsequently during the 1960s publicised the ideas of others. A broad and catholic spectrum of writers including Basil Bernstein, Royston Lambert, Edward de Bono, Patrick McGeeney, Michael Young and, of course, Brian Jackson himself were among those whose ideas were introduced to a wider public through its pages. ACE also thrust many of these ideas at the mass media for further dilution but greater dissemination.[8]

This in turn helped to publicise the work of ACE. One such article, based on the researches of John Wakeford, was published as a supplement in February 1964. It attacked the public schools for not delivering GCE 'A'-level passes in a cost-effective way. It brought huge publicity to *Where?* when it was taken up by the *Sunday Times.* The circulation of *Where?* got a massive boost, and the membership of ACE increased substantially.[9]

Brian was also concerned to identify gaps in the educational system and to lobby for their rectification. A good example of his work in this field is the clearing house he set up, again in conjunction with the *Sunday Times* to publicise vacancies and find places on degree courses at technical colleges for thousands of students who were unable, despite having good-enough qualifications, to get into universities.

Kathleen Hartley joined the expanding ACE team in late 1962 and took over as the Secretary from Sonia Abrams when she moved to research in the following summer. She found some 5,000 such students existed but she also discovered 1,260 empty places and believed there were at least another thousand. ACE urged that technical colleges should publicise their degree courses more positively and that there should be a unified Clearing House for admission to higher education. This report received a vast amount of publicity, drew shoals of favourable comments, prompted questions in Parliament, and official statements of interest. Yet nothing happened. Twelve months passed and deciding it was pointless to waste any more time with the Ministry of Education the people at ACE decided to shame the authorities by setting up their own Clearing House. They collected information on vacancies from the colleges by telephone each Friday and the *Sunday Times* ran a weekly feature spotlighting these opportunities. Over the ten-week period of running the Clearing House some 2,000 students contacted ACE but still there was no response from officialdom. Therefore in 1965 ACE dusted off its Clearing House kit and that year reached 4,000 students despite being refused any help from the Ministry. After repeating the exercise in 1966 when, again with the vigorous help of the *Sunday Times* they reached about 5,000 students, the 'sheer craziness of it pierced Curzon Street'.[10] Yet the first Brian Jackson knew that the Ministry, or Department of Education and Science as it had by then become, had decided to run an official clearing house in 1967, was when he read it in the paper. No one even informed ACE, let alone tried to tap their expertise. The resulting service, which the DES paid ACE to monitor, was so poor that they felt obliged, in response to large numbers of enquiries, to run the service with the *Sunday Times* for a final year in 1968 before handing the job to the authorities as had been their avowed intention all along. As Brian said, when ACE felt it had to go beyond giving advice and publicity to taking action to plug a perceived gap, then as soon as possible 'Our job must be to work ourselves out of our job.'[11]

Brian was also actively involved with pioneering the Dawn University. This was an early experiment in using television as a teaching tool. It was intended as a pilot scheme for a University of the Air and was launched by ACE with the help of Peter Laslett and Anglia Television – the BBC at that stage was less than enthusiastic – in the summer of 1963. Its success led to the foundation by ACE of the National Extension College NEC which was to be the role-model in due course for the Open University and will be discussed in a separate chapter.[12] .

It was during his years at ACE that Brian began actively to campaign for the rights and well-being of a group that was to become in subsequent years his main pre-occupation: the under-fives. Michael Young, as chairman of ACE, was appointed to Lady Plowden's committee which was to investigate pre-school, and primary, education. Brian was thus able to lobby the committee constantly and with considerable success. Indeed in 1967 the Plowden Report referred flatteringly to the work of ACE:

> The growing interest in informed help on educational matters is shown by the response to an Advisory centre which publishes a magazine every two months and answers queries by post. . . .To meet the demand [for information] an Advice Bureau was run for seven days in a department store in a large town. The experiment was thought to

be justified by the interest and enthusiasm of the questioners, their frequent ignorance of the way the educational system worked and the relief they showed at receiving support for their ambitions or reassurance that their problem was not unusual or insoluble.[13]

The advice bureau referred to was the Education Shop set up in Ipswich Co-op's central store in October 1965. Brian Jackson fully recognised that the readership of *Where?* was predominantly the literate and numerate middle class, including people involved in education as well as parents, and that it was in danger of broadening rather than narrowing the gap between the educationally advantaged children of such parents and their working-class fellows. He rationalised this uncomfortably non-socialist position by the belief that ACE was strengthening the hand of those members of society whose actions at local level would be of benefit to the community at large.[14] Nevertheless, he constantly sought to broaden his audience. The Education Shop was an attempt to reach the parents who would never read *Where?*

The Plowden Report not only recommended the greater involvement of parents in their children's education, a major *Where?* platform, but also identified areas it described as of 'educational priority' and was, according to Willem van der Eyken, 'rightly concerned to see pre-school places provided for children [in them]'.[15] Having got so much of ACE's policy endorsed by Plowden it seemed a good idea to publicise the committee's report as widely and as quickly as possible. Peter Preston had been education correspondent, in those days a somewhat rare creature, for the *Guardian* and he wrote a summary of the report – *Plowden for Parents* – for ACE. Brian had the knack of finding the right people and persuading them to help in an emergency. As he wrote to Peter Preston 'Many congratulations . . . wouldn't have done it if you hadn't agreed . . . couldn't be more efficient to work with . . .marvellous to see it turned into fact so speedily. . . .'[16]

Brian was rarely content just to disseminate ideas, or even to lobby for their acceptance. He always wanted to *do* something; to be *involved*. As a result, under the auspices of ACE, he set up the Association of Multi-Racial Playgroups in conjunction with the Indian Workers' Association and the Race-Relations Committee of the Society of Friends. In turn, this became the Priority Area Playgroup project.

The project started in Birmingham in 1967 and was established by Brian in partnership with the immigrant – mostly Asian – community, but also working closely with the host community, voluntary workers and officials. Announcing the project in *Where?* number 31 in May 1967 Brian referred to a previous ACE scheme to set up a low-cost do-it-yourself playgroup in Cambridge but admitted that the participants had been articulate middle-class parents whose children were possibly those least in need of pre-school stimulation outside the home. The Birmingham project was intended to see if the scheme could work in a deprived area. As always with ACE projects, the aim was to show the way, through self-help groups, but ultimately to withdraw once a project was under way and especially if by then it had established itself with government or local government funding aid.

Nevertheless the Birmingham project was to have an extra dimension. Thanks largely to the co-operation and initiative of the BBC producer David Gretton, the nursery was to be televised and shown nation-wide on Gretton's pioneering programme for Asian immigrants *Apna Hi Ghar Samajhiye* (Make yourself at home). Sadly Gretton died shortly after the Van Leer Foundation had agreed to fund the project for a year and the school was called the David Gretton Nursery in his memory.[17]

There were plenty of problems for the new organisation. In the first place they felt the playgroup had to approximate as nearly as possible to a good state nursery class. This meant finding permanent premises and a stiffening of paid teachers together with lots of play material, all of which cost money. Secondly there was the need to reconcile differing cultures; the group was not intended merely to be a liberal outpost of middle-class life. For example it suggested that Asian festivals such as Divali should be celebrated as well as Pancake Tuesday. Yet, as Brian discovered, West Indian and Asian children and their parents did not share our European culture of play as a learning activity. Although this was fundamental to the concept of playgroups ACE had to modify its approach accordingly. A third problem, partly linked to this, was that for different reasons the local community, both English manual workers and immigrant families, did not particularly want a playgroup, let alone the responsibility of running it themselves.

Nevertheless the project was started. Joan Jones, a Birmingham health visitor was seconded to it and Mrs Meher Khan was appointed as teacher in charge. An Indian voluntary assistant teacher left after a short time because of difficulties between the Indian and Pakistani groups associated with the project and was replaced by an untrained assistant, Marie Kindon.[18] Eventually, after the first parents' committee had voted to increase the fees and then withdrawn its children the following term, a second committee was established and, in due course, the whole project was taken over by a local committee of parents and teachers with co-opted representatives of the local authority, the BBC, ACE, and the Pre-School Playgroups Association, under the chairmanship of Dr Dhani Prem.[19]

Brian gave a rather blunt description of the difficulties experienced in Birmingham in an internal report.[20] After a good start with an £8,000 grant, Joan Jones seconded, TV link-up, official opening by Dennis Howell, he wrote, 'came the sticky period.'[21] Relations between Cambridge and Birmingham deteriorated, local immigrant leaders were pro-Joan, who was already known to them, but anti-ACE. Brian had to take back responsibility for the project and conciliate with the help of Ruby Rae, a sociological researcher from Cambridge. There was also a rift between the project and the

BBC who had their own troubles: the original contact, David Bryson had left and his replacement apparently went off for three months with a nervous breakdown. And finally, the local authority refused to take over financial responsibility after the grant ran out. As a result, Brian reported, 'Van Leer got shirty and bad relations resulted'.[22] There was almost certainly a personal element in this situation too. Brian's charm could sometimes work rather too well so that women frequently became victims of their own misreading of his position.[23] This situation could be exacerbated by his being extremely possessive – a 'control freak' as one woman has described him.[24] The friction between Brian and Mrs Jones appears to have been a classic example of this.

Despite all these setbacks the school must be counted a success. It spawned other groups: the Indian Ladies Club in 1967 and the Association of Pakistani Women in 1968. In due course a further ten playgroups were set up in and around Birmingham.[25] And yet in a sense it failed to achieve its primary objective. Although it and its spin-offs came to fruition in areas designated as deprived according to various statistics taken from the 1966 census, they were functioning under the auspices of an Asian immigrant community that was essentially middle class. The indigenous white working class played almost no part. Brian learned something fundamental as a result of this project: he discovered that the reason West Indian children were not attending, despite their proliferation in the communities concerned, was that their mothers were out at work and they were with child minders from 7am to 7pm. The nursery was quite unable to provide care for such a long period.[26]

ACE's endeavours, then, were not always successful. For every project that came to fruition, frequently like the playgroups only after a great struggle, there were many that were still-born or that fizzled out after a promising start.

One such project started with an article in *Where?* in October 1965 written by Harry Ree, then Professor of Education at the newly founded University of York. He suggested that a register should be formed of retired teachers who would be prepared to come out of retirement to alleviate the shortage of teachers – partly the result of the post-war baby boom – and to free younger teachers for refresher courses. Brian took up the idea and sent a copy of the article to the Minister of Education offering ACE's services to implement and co-ordinate the scheme. The Minister turned it down; for one thing, he said, teachers could not draw their pensions *and* earn money at the same time. Brian thought this a mealy-mouthed excuse and a less-than-amicable correspondence ensued.[27] Meanwhile Brian tried to fly the idea via the *Daily Mail* but they turned it down too. Eventually Brian gave up. He wrote to Ree on 17 December 1965 'I think it is pretty hopeless trying to persuade this bloke Prentice to do anything'.[28] Harry Ree had had a distinguished career in espionage during World War II and was an important figure in the educational world but a decidedly eccentric character.[29] During the above correspondence he wrote to Brian on 26 November 1965 'I'd like to get Shirley Williams or

Irene Ward to bite Prentice's leg. . .'. Ree had been strongly criticised in *Education and the Working Class* when as headmaster of Watford Grammar School in 1953 he maintained in a letter to the *Times Educational Supplement* that very few potential graduates were leaving school at sixteen, the majority of them having already 'approached their academic ceiling'. Brian's comment was that he 'could hardly have been more experienced or more wrong.'[30] Harry Ree became a great friend to Brian and wrote an introduction to the posthumous edition of *Education and the Working Class* (1986) in which he acknowledged the criticism and said 'I owe much to Brian'. His biography of the pioneer educationalist, Henry Morris, includes a juicy selection of Morris's more robust views with which both he and Brian were broadly in sympathy.[31] Always rather unconventional – he was once barely restrained by his wife from serving guests fruit salad on their used dinner plates – he later gave up his chair at York to 'go back to the chalk face' and teach at a secondary school in the East End of London.[32]

Another project, the Home and School Council, was launched in response to Plowden, with great publicity on 20 November 1967 at the Waldorf Hotel. There were twenty-four journalists from all the major papers in attendance. Sonia Jackson was to be its director and she was to be funded for three years by the Joseph Rowntree Charitable Trust. The Home and School Council was formed as a result of the huge response to an article by Michael Young in the *Observer* 5 November 1967 entitled 'Getting Parents to Schools'.[33] Young pointed out that the appointment of parent-governors was one of the Plowden ideas that would cost the taxpayer nothing and he wrote to all chief education officers urging their support. The original idea was hatched back in January 1967 between Brian and Michael Young who wrote a joint letter to *Where?* which appeared in the March issue.[34] Brian reported later to Sonia how he and Michael Young had met two representatives of the Confederation for the Advancement of State Education, CASE, and two from the National Confederation of Parent-Teacher Associations: 'We agreed, it took hours, to form a Home and School Council, not much more than a name and quarterly meetings at first, but we'd start off by issuing common statements when needed and doing common lobbying of the education Minister'. The letter continues. 'Both said when they saw Crosland his first automatic question was "But surely you're quite unrepresentative?" and Brian then outlined plans to raise money for a field officer and expressed a hope that the Council would be based on ACE 'Who will almost certainly take it over and a good thing too – all solemn men in suits sitting around a table, they seemed happy to settle there for the whole day. . . .'[35]

Money was raised for the Home and School Council and Robert Finch, a 32-year old assistant master at Uppingham School was appointed Field Officer and based at Derwent College, University of York. Sonia wrote about the aims of the council in *Where?* in January 1968. Articles appeared in *The*

Times Educational Supplement and *New Society* in October 1968 publicising 'Home and School Day' which was an idea of the Council, and an Education Shop which CASE ran in Richmond-on-Thames in conjunction with 'Home and School Week'.[36] Yet after all this, in his progress report in 1970 Brian only mentions briefly that it was 'a coming-together of the three main bodies representing active parents', and in an internal report at the same time he said of the Council there was little activity.[37] There had been signs of disharmony almost from the start. The article in *New Society* had already suggested that the Council suffered from a split personality being both political and therapeutic and pointing out that while PTAs were locally-based both ACE and CASE were national, the former being the information getter and the latter the real pressure group. By and large, it said, the Council needed to learn from the work of CASE. Home and School was also the title given to the regular column which ACE ran fortnightly for three years courtesy of the *Guardian.*[38] What appears to have happened is that ACE was instrumental in launching the Council and brought both CASE, the proponents of state education, and the National Confederation of Parent-Teacher Associations together, albeit somewhat reluctantly. A letter on the latter's headed paper in July 1969 refers to the council as 'dominated by articulate and clever' (people at ACE) and is less than complimentary about CASE. ACE relinquished any control it may have had over the Home and School Council in September 1969.[39] Its sad progress or rather lack of progress was succinctly described by M. Locke in 1974 in *Power and Politics in the School System.*

> The Home and School Council is much less than it was originally
> intended to be. Established in 1967 it was inspired by a vision of one
> great association representing and linking parents and teachers. It
> was a vision largely of ACE's Chairman, Michael Young, and Director,
> Brian Jackson. There was a hope that CASE and the NCPTA would be
> able to dissolve their identities into one body, but rivalry and suspicion
> that ACE was empire-building combined with the different interest
> of parent and teacher associations combined to wreck the idea. . . .

Since the Home and School Council deflated, there have been a few attempts to revive the vision. Brian Jackson wrote in the *Home and School Newsletter* (September 1971): 'What we badly need in the next decade is a National Union of Parents and Pupils which will be party to decisions affecting their interests, as the teachers are party to ones affecting theirs.' It would be formed out of ACE, CASE, and the NCPTA. He was writing in support of an article proposing a parents' union which would take its place alongside the teacher unions in national debate and consultations about educational policy. The next issue of the newsletter was to have contained a report of reactions to this proposal, but, after it had been printed certain people in the parent-teacher movement were so offended by some remarks slighting them that the whole article had to be torn out before the newsletter was distributed. Such is the politics of pressure groups.[40]

Another example of a project that failed to get off the ground was the proposed Birmingham Home School Development Unit which Brian outlined in a draft dated October 1967. The plan was to follow up recommendations in Plowden to implement positive discrimination in priority areas – inner-city areas of deprivation – by a wide programme of action research. The idea was to set up self-help schemes for parents and then monitor them. It was to be based on the David Gretton Nursery which was already in existence. Brian had assembled a formidable research committee at ACE and in a circular dated 3 January 1968 he summed up his aims as follows; 'First get the money and support while still keeping the brief as open as possible'. He then listed his subsequent tasks as; '1. identify cultural strengths in EPA [Educational Priority Area], 2. test them in pre-school learning situations, 3. begin to translate them into a teaching strategy, a pedagogy, 4. get them over hurdles [into infant school, transfer to junior school etc.], 5. evaluate them as well as we can, as it goes along.'[41] Sadly the next item in the file is a letter to the Van Leer Foundation which refers to a visit from the 'Ford people', but they won't fund it so 'I'm afraid, Henry, that our hopes rest with your Trustees. . .'.[42] There is no reply in the file. Unabashed, Brian was drafting a proposal the following month for a Priority Area Information Service to be based on the Home and School Council which 'focuses the action of parent bodies in furthering Plowden's recommendations on the relationship between home and school.'[43]

A major function of the Advisory Centre for Education was, naturally enough, the giving of advice or rather since it had to pay its way, the sale of advice. Apparently ACE never encouraged parents to send their problems in but they did so right from the start.[44] In the early 1960s it was possible for one well-informed educationalist to field almost any problem that parents were likely to ask. Indeed one such man did just that.[45] Leonard White was then Borough Education Officer for Gosport. He was a barrister and an expert in the law of education and was recruited by Young from the start to extend the advice service he gave to parents in Gosport. He later joined the council of ACE and was its Vice-Chairman from January 1966 to the time of his death. Between 1966 and 1971 he contributed more than twenty articles on a wide range of legal topics from safety and punishment to 'What to do if your children's teacher has a breakdown', or 'Who can take the school bus?'. ACE published these as a book, *Parents and Law,* in 1972. Len White died 9 September 1973 and ACE, who in early 1969 had moved into Fitzwilliam House, a rather grand Queen Anne building at 32 Trumpington Street, Cambridge, decided to rename it Dr White House in his memory. Only one voice was raised to suggest it might be preferable to call the place Leonard White House, but this was overruled by the committee. It is apt that at the same meeting there was discussion of the criticisms that the profiles of the new ACE Council in a recent edition of *Where?* had provoked. These were that there were no women and that many of the men were too old to be parents of schoolchildren.[46]

As the title of Brian's report on the Advisory Service, *100,000 Questions* confirms, the questions kept coming and their nature became more complex as education itself expanded during the decade. Ann Newton joined ACE in Autumn 1963 to help run the service and in May 1966 Richard Blake became its new head. By November of that year Michael Bird was introduced by *Where?* as Director of Information only to be succeeded in July 1967 by Michael McGarth. In January 1968 Jo Rawlings took over as head of the service and by 1970 there were four advisors at work on it.

The range of topics arriving in ACE's post was huge and varied. Some, like 'how to choose a school?' occurred daily while others cropped up only once a year. Some were specific and some, like 'how to raise a two-year-old child?', were quite general.[47] ACE did a survey of every letter received during two weeks of June 1970. Out of 232 enquiries 28 simply sought information such as names of publications or addresses. These were answered free. Over the years ACE had produced various booklets on specific recurring problems and there were 55 straightforward orders for these. In order to provide inside, though admittedly highly subjective, information on schools nation-wide, ACE had initiated a Parent to Parent service which invited its subscribers to send reports on their own children's schools. There were eleven orders for copies of these. A further 35 letters received one of nine standard replies, also free. These covered such topics as the eleven-plus examination, higher education, and the problems of children with handicaps; especially dyslexia which many schools at that time did not recognise. The remaining 106 (sic) paid-up questions at 10s (50p) each were split roughly into three areas: day school, boarding school, and higher education, representing as Brian was acutely aware a very middle-class readership.

It was always felt at ACE that each of these questions represented a vote of no confidence in the advice given, or *not* given, by the authorities and that *they* not ACE should be providing the answers. So, rather than simply type out thousands of replies, which would have done nothing to prevent the same problems arising again for other parents, students, or teachers, they tried when they found particular problems arising time and time again to find a better solution.

The Parent to Parent service described above was one such response as was the Technical College Vacancy Scheme mentioned earlier. The latter, in addition to its free service courtesy of the *Sunday Times,* offered an information pack which for 10s 6d (52p) included an individual vacancy list, details of all degree and diploma courses in technical colleges, including London University external degree courses, and information on grants. Over 20,000 of these were sold during the five years ACE ran the service.

Although Brian was pleased to be able to report a substantial decline in requests for information on higher education during the late 1960s it was still obvious that what universities and colleges put in their glossy brochures was not always what sixth-formers wanted. So ACE launched Sixteen Plus. For two years, 1967-68, they took a total of fifteen subjects and sought answers to such questions as size of course, proportion of applicants admitted in the previous year, failure rate, possibility of transfer to other courses after the first year, and so forth. These were the sorts of details that Robbins had in mind when proposing a National Information Service on Higher Education. The failure rate of students admitted was as much a concern of Brian's as the failure of students to find places. He wrote on the subject in *Where?* in 1965 and eventually published a league table of universities whose students dropped out.[48] In its short life, according to Brian, Sixteen Plus created a new atmosphere and a change of attitude by universities with many departments responding enthusiastically to the opportunity to give the facts about their courses. Again, as with the Clearing House scheme for admission to higher education, ACE had identified a problem, shown what might be done, and thereby encouraged the universities to provide a better service.

ACE's main way of disseminating information and advice was, however, always through the national press. This relationship was, to a large extent, symbiotic. When ACE was founded in 1960 *The Times* did not have an education correspondent, and as late as 1968 there were only fourteen correspondents for education to cover 23 national news organisations, as compared to 33 labour and 46 lobby correspondents.[49] Yet both junior and secondary schools were undergoing major changes, and arguments about the nature of education were a major topic of interest, at least to what some might now call the 'chattering classes'. The need for information was met by Brian and his colleagues and, as interest in education grew and education itself became more complex, a snowball effect was created and an increasing awareness of the need for advice led to even greater opportunities for ACE to get its messages across to an ever-wider audience. The newspapers eventually decided that education was important. Education correspondents became almost a craze and at least one of them from those days, Peter Preston, went on to much greater things.[50] Syndication provided the biggest opportunity for *Where?*, with one series running to 150 articles and although most were published in local evening newspapers enquiries were prompted from as far afield as Australia, South Africa, and Hong Kong.

Running short residential courses was also part of the business of ACE. As early as 1961 they had held a summer school.[51] In July 1967 Stan Dennis, who had been in charge or the Clearing House Scheme took over respons-ibility for these courses and in October 1967 Kathleen Hartley, who was then Executive Director, was able to report that eight of the nine courses planned for January 1968 were going ahead.[52] Many of the courses were refresher courses for teachers, or courses relating to changes in educational policy

Barrie Knight (in bow tie) and Brian Jackson with freinds.

and in response to government legislation and proposed legislation. Though never a major part of ACE's activities – shortage of suitable staff was one problem – they contributed modestly to ACE's income. A course on teaching unstreamed classes for 128 teachers in January 1970 made a profit – Brian used the word *surplus* – of £220.[53]

As the 1960s closed ACE ended its first ten years as a firmly established institution in the world of education. In 1969 ACE had made its first *surplus* or profit, proving that it was at last viable, though the future looked less rosy with costs rising and little opportunity to expand in terms of membership or new ventures.[54] It had seen great growth and many changes of personnel, often as a result of promotion to other work within ACE. When Sasha Young gave up editing *Where?* after her baby was born Sonia Abrams and later Kathleen Hartley took on the job. She was replaced in March 1966 by Beryl McAlhone who continued well into the next decade. Richard Blake, was appointed in May 1966 as head of the Advisory Service with a brief from Brian to establish a regular column in the *Guardian*. He eventually became executive director in the autumn of 1968, when Dick Freeman took over the column. Blake stayed at ACE eight years and was to play a key role there and, later, in both Priority and the NEC. He introduced Eric Midwinter to Brian, thus instigating a hugely fruitful partnership and a friendship that lasted to the end of Brian's life. In addition his was the dubious distinction of having introduced Brian to Barrie Knight, a charming, though rather flamboyant former bookmaker's employee who was Richard's neighbour and later became Brian's right-hand man and drinking companion. Richard described his unease at what he saw as Brian's unorthodox interviewing technique but admits he was delighted when, after chatting to him for half an hour and introducing him to the existing members of staff, Brian looked at him sideways somewhat quizzically and said quietly, 'You know Richard, we've had forty applicants for this job. But you're the best. When can you start?'[55] It was enough to make anyone feel good, whatever the truth of the matter.

In less than ten years Brian Jackson had rescued ACE and built it into an important body, not only for disseminating information, but also for lobbying to bring about improvements in services and information provided by schools and universities themselves. In addition to influencing the Plowden committee's recommendations he had been actively involved in showing how self-help groups could provide pre-school educational facilities even in poorer inner-city areas. He had helped create a much wider interest in educational matters in the press generally and, not least, by his enthusiasm and charisma he had built a strong and informed team to take ACE into the next decade. He had, in short, transformed ACE from a good idea to a viable, independent, national force.

Meanwhile Brian and Sonia were on the move; first in September 1968 to 352 Hills Road Cambridge where her children, Dominic, 10, and Rebecca, 5 joined them. Brian's children, Christian, 7, and Lucy, 5 remained with their mother who subsequently went to live with Philip Abrams and then moved with him to Durham. In January 1969 Brian and Sonia rented the Black Bull in Landbeach, a small village a few miles north of Cambridge. The Black Bull, as its name implies, was a former public house. It is a charming old building with a large garden: an idyllic place for the children. They were to have five happy years there during which time their first child would be born.

Although Brian remained Director of ACE throughout this period he was, of course, simultaneously building up the National Extension College, publishing various books including the very influential *Streaming* in 1964, teaching English to Cambridge undergraduates, and writing articles and reviewing books in a wide variety of newspapers and magazines. These and other professional activities will form the subject of subsequent chapters.

Notes

1. Michael Young 'A tribute to Brian Jackson', *Where?*, September 1983.
2. Judith Bridgeman (*née* Baker), 'Brian Jackson: an ACE educator' (unpublished project, Homerton College, 1972).
3. John Henniker, sometime director of the Wates Foundation, in a letter to the writer, 12 August 1993.
4. Michael Young, *Where?*, September 1983.
5. Brian Jackson, 'Schools fit for a Princess', *Guardian*, 24 July 1963, p.8.
6. *Where?*, Summer 1962.
7. Brian Jackson, *1960-1970 A Progress Report*, p.3.
8. *Ibid.*, p.4.
9. Interview with Sonia Jackson, 16 August 1993.
10. Brian Jackson, *1960-1970 A Progress Report*, p.12.
11. *Ibid.*, p.8.
12. Michael Young, *Where?*, September 1983, p.3.
13. *Children and their Primary Schools*, commonly known as the *Plowden Report*, p.1.

14. Brian Jackson, *1960-1970 A Progress Report*, p.8.
15. Willem van der Eyken, *The Pre-School Years*, p.155.
16. Letter to Peter Preston, 20 March 1967, F3.
17. Brian uses both the terms 'school' and 'nursery' in his various reports. I have followed his usage.
18. Brian Jackson and Ruby Rae, 'Priority Playgroups', *Where?*, January 1970, pp.18-21.
19. *Idem.*
20. Brian Jackson, 'Report on the Birmingham Project', 31 January 1969, MS, E9.
21. *Idem.*
22. *Idem.*
23. Discussion with Hazel Wigmore, 28 May 1993.
24. Interview with Julia Rackowe (McGawley), 16 October 1996.
25. Brian Jackson and Ruby Rae, 'Priority Playgroups', *Where?*, January 1970, p.21.
26. *Idem.*
27. Letters, Brian Jackson/Harry Ree/Roy Nash, October-December 1965, C9.
28. *Idem.*
29. I am indebted to my supervisor, Professor Keith Laybourn, for background information on Harry Ree.
30. Jackson and Marsden, *Education and the Working Class*, p.218.
31. Review by Brian Jackson of *Educator Extrordinary*, MS, F6.
32. Interview with Sonia Jackson, 16 August 1993.
33. Report by Sonia (Abrams) Jackson, MS, C6
34. Brian Jackson, letter to Sonia Abrams, 30 January 1967.
35. Brian Jackson. Letter to Sonia Abrams, 18 April 1967.
36. 'Extra Open Day' *New Society*, 10 October 1968,'Boutique with a difference', *The Times Educational Supplement*, 11 October 1968.
37. Brian Jackson, Report to ACE Council, 25 March 1970, MS, F1.
38. Brian Jackson, *100,000 Questions*, p.17.
39. Brian Jackson, 'Who does ACE serve?', *Where?* No.45, September 1969.
40. M. Locke, *Power and Politics in the School System*, pp. 50-51.
41. Circular on the Birmingham Scheme, MS, C6.
42. Brian Jackson, Draft Proposal, MS, C6.
43. *Ibid.*
44. Brian Jackson, *100,000 Questions*, p.1. I have taken much of what follows about the advisory service from this booklet.
45. Interview with Sonia Jackson, 16 August 1993. Also Michael Young, 'ACE Has a New Council', *Where?*, August 1973, pp.230-231.
46. Minutes of meeting of ACE executive committee, 2 October 1973, MS, F1.
47. *100,000 Questions*, p.3.
48. Brian Jackson, 'Students who fail', *Where?*, Spring 1965.
49. Jeremy Tunstall, 'The education correspondents', *New Society*, 27 August 1970, quoted in *100,000 Questions*.
50. Interview with Paul Barker, 6 June 1997.
51. *Where?*, Summer 1961.
52. *Where?*, July 1967, Kathleen Hartley, Report to ACE Management Committee, October 1967, MS, F1.
53. Brian Jackson, Report to ACE Council, 25 March 1970, MS, F1.
54. *Idem.*
55. Interview with Richard Blake, 23 September 1994.

Chapter 3
The National Extension College
and the Open University

The late Lord Wilson of Rievaulx once claimed to have dreamt up the Open University, 'Between church and lunch I wrote the whole outline of a proposal for a University of the Air' on Easter Sunday morning in the Isles of Scilly in 1963.[1] And, indeed, he will be remembered as having given it substance: *The Times* obituary of Lord Wilson said 'Perhaps his most enduring and characteristic achievement . . . was the founding of the Open University.'[2] But as Brian Jackson wrote: 'it wasn't like that'. Indeed, although Wilson aired the idea in a speech in Glasgow later that year on 8 September – according to some cynics only to give the national press a non-Scottish headline – there was no mention of a University of the Air in the Labour Party manifesto for the 1964 general election.[3]

It has been said that 'The Open University owes its existence as much to [Brian Jackson] as to anyone else' and there are those who would even say *more* than anyone else.[4] Brian wrote in 1979,

> Before the conversion of Sir Harold, the essence of the idea was to revivify the tradition of James Stuart [who started the Extra-Mural Boards], Canon Barnett [who saw Toynbee Hall as the 'University of the East End'], R.H. Tawney [who prompted the Workers' Educational Association], and marry correspondence, radio, television, and tutorials to help the underprivileged. It was about equality. At the Advisory Centre for Education we had not only published the idea – under the name of Open University – but very actively lobbied it. and largely with John Scupham's help, set up a string of pilot schemes with the BBC, and a Dawn University trial with the IBA.[5]

Michael Young reported that 'one crucial moment was in 1960' when Brian met him on the steps of 'that dreadful building', the University Library in Cambridge.

> I had been there preparing a lecture. It was sunny. We sat on the steps. He said 'What are you going to do next?'. 'And you Brian?' He urged me not to get absorbed by the comfortable haven of Cambridge and do something like starting a new university. He said he would help.'[6]

Young continues the story, 'within a few months we had organised the first ever summer school for external degree students from London University and, with the marvellous support of Peter Laslett, persuaded Anglia Television to put on the first *Dawn University*.'[7]

Laslett himself referred to the episode as one of Brian's disappointments:

'the most important venture of all in which [Brian Jackson] and Michael Young and I were all associated . . . the attempt to get the Open University created out of the National Extension College. . .'. He concluded that 'this has meant that Brian Jackson has yet to receive the recognition he so much deserves in this, as in so much else, and surely will receive as his career goes on.'[8]

What is not in doubt is that Brian single-handedly set up the National Extension College, NEC, nursed it through its teething troubles, supervised its sudden and almost involuntary absorption of the University Correspondence College, rescued it from disaster during the postal strike of 1971 and re-launched it with hand-picked staff from ACE to become the thriving enterprise it remains today. Although, when the Labour Government eventually launched the Open University, Jenny Lee ignored the NEC, the story of its development is worth repeating. It illustrates so many of Brian's methods and talents and, although there may be other claimants to parentage of the OU, at least one former member of that government shares my view that the NEC was 'a very important milestone in [its] development.[9]

After Harold Wilson's Glasgow speech in September 1963 the following month's *Where?* carried an article by Michael Young noting that 'so far nothing has been done', and announcing the birth of the National Extension College.

> Ours will be the invisible college of Cambridge. With no college buildings of its own, it will use university and other premises, in the vacations, both in and out of Cambridge. With no full-time teachers of its own, its first staff will be from the universities of Cambridge, Keele, Bristol, Harvard and Hull, as well as from the remarkable College of Arts and Technology in Cambridge. Without any official grant, its equipment will come mainly from the sort of far-sighted people in industry who supported nineteenth-century civic industries. . . .[10]

In fact its rather grandiose name was the most impressive thing about the new institution. Its home was a tiny back room in a condemned workman's cottage next to a pub in Russell Street, Cambridge. Michael Young was Chairman and its Director, Brian Jackson and Treasurer, Howard Dickinson were also shared with ACE.

It had one staff member of its own, David Grugeon. He was a London teacher who was seconded for a year as Administrator, or as he put it later in a letter to Brian, 'as stooge to act the part'.[11] He claimed his only contribution was to spot an article in the *Guardian* about the Pre-School Playgroups people 'pinching' a New Zealand correspondence course on how to set up a playgroup and suggesting that the NEC take it up. He concluded that he was sorry for the people at NEC (now) as they have to fulfil what Michael Young, Brian Jackson and he promised.

The original funding of the NEC was on a small scale. Brian applied for and obtained a combined loan and grant of £20,000 from the Calouste Gulbenkian Foundation.[12] There was also a smaller grant from the Elmgrant Trust of Dartington Hall, and £1,000 contributed by *Guardian* readers. Nevertheless the new College offered a wide range of planned activities covering further as well as higher education. Its playgroup course complemented one for mothers, including graduates, wishing to train as teachers – there was a shortage of teachers at that time as the 'baby boom' of the 1940s worked its way through school – while 'O' level courses in English and maths with linked broadcasts, business mathematics and electronics, catered for academic and professional needs. A language bus, funded by the owners of the local electronics firm Pye, offering French by tape recorder and a radio-construction kit were aimed at the youth and the adult-leisure markets. In higher education the college proposed residential courses and a tutorial scheme for external degree students of London University.

In the same month as NEC was founded came the first experiments in televising university lectures which ACE sponsored for Cambridge Television Week. In the 'Dawn University' run in partnership with Anglia Television and Independent Television (ITV), Professor Fred Hoyle led off at 7.15 am on Monday 21 October 1963 with 'The Mathematics of Violence' which was followed through the following days by lectures on molecular biology, psychology, engineering and English. Although these transmissions anticipated the antisocial hours of subsequent Open University broadcasting they attracted a large audience. Follow-up research by Peter Jenner commissioned by the ITV showed some 200,000 people – nearly twice the university population of Great Britain at the time, as Brian commented, – had watched and furthermore they were exactly the audience the NEC was looking for: 'a young audience, made up in some part of men and women who wanted university education but couldn't get it.'[13]

This flurry of publicity accompanying the launch of the NEC brought 'enquiries, donations and expressions of goodwill from all over the world. Some 3,000 potential students wrote for details of NEC courses in the first eight weeks, including 600 married women interested in the teacher-training and playgroup leader courses.'[14] It had been a heady beginning so typical of Brian's capacity to conceive on a grand scale and, after announcing the concept as a reality, to conjure its substance seemingly from the air itself. Recognition was soon forthcoming. The *Guardian* carried a leader on 18 September 1964 which announced 'the Advisory Centre for Education's plans for a National Extension College are now rapidly taking shape . . . we should all be grateful to the college for this important pioneering work, leading towards ACE's vision of the 'Open University' – certainly a better name than Mr Harold Wilson's original 'University of the Air' since much of the work must necessarily be done on the ground. . .'. A few months later Anthony Crosland, then Secretary of State for Education and Science, said in Douglas, Isle of Man in April 1965 *a propos* the re-training of married women as teachers; 'I am exceedingly grateful for the efforts of . . . the NEC'[15] Very shortly Brian was to exercise his other great talent; that of creating and motivating a team to carry out his grandiose schemes, for the NEC was to take on large responsibilities much sooner than anyone could have imagined.

One of Brian's aims in founding the NEC was to raise the standards of correspondence colleges. A Consumer's Association survey published in *Which?* to coincide with the launch of the NEC showed that most of them were privately owned profit-making bodies whose standards were appallingly low and whose courses were often duplicated and drearily uninspiring. As Michael Young pointed out in *Where?,* they made more profit from people who gave up the courses they had paid for in advance than from those who successfully completed them. Brian campaigned long and hard for the independent accreditation of these colleges but in vain. He was still writing, hectoringly, but to no avail, in 1968 to the Minister of Education Edward Short who replied that he 'regrets he cannot go along with your [Brian's] demand for independent accreditation of correspondence colleges'.[16] One long-established and rather dull correspondence college was not a profit-making enterprise. The rather grandly named University Correspondence College, UCC, was based in Cambridge where it had been established by a university teacher, William Briggs, in 1887. It was a charity and had flourished until the late 1940s. H.G. Wells had once been on its staff and was said to have written *The Time Machine* in his office there overlooking Parker's Piece.[17] But by the early 1960s it was losing money. Its trustees were reluctant to close it down as the college always had students in mid course. Instead they hit on the brilliant idea of backing it, to use a stock-market term, lock, stock, and barrel into the newly-formed NEC. Hilary Perraton who became NEC's first educational director in 1965 described the free gift thus:

> We acquired a red-brick Victorian terrace, furniture which must have gone back to the nineteenth century and a diverse array of courses. . . . The building was less of an asset than it sounds for the lease was about to fall in and the terrace had as many staircases as an unconvincing whodunit. Along with the building we inherited the goodwill, a nucleus of staff, and the accounts for the previous fifty years. The courses had their interest for they betrayed the origins of the [movement. . . . They were still] offering courses on a very individual basis, far removed from the mass production of teaching materials which is the basis of the Open University's – and, for that matter, the NEC's – whole economy.[18]

The result of this merger was to influence the future development of the NEC in three quite dramatic ways. It had inherited some 3,000 students and it had to re-vamp their courses both quickly and drastically – academic assessors gave an almost universal thumbs-down to courses at degree and GEC level as well as those for professional qualifications – as it was clear that their fees for such examinable study would be the bread and butter of the college's income.

That income was necessary because, secondly, the NEC had inherited about fifty new employees and whilst many retired, or resigned thankfully after the merger, the rest were needed and had to be paid. Thirdly there was a small financial windfall in that the UCC had shares in the University Tutorial Press and the sale of these provided a cash float that was used to finance the necessary restructuring of course material over the next couple of years. It also sold back the lease on its Victorian pile to the Cambridge council who wanted to demolish it to build a multi-storey car park.[19]

Thus by 1968 the NEC had metamorphosed in five years from an idealistic dream into an up-to-date and fully functioning correspondence college, with some 7,000 students taking courses from a range of 26 'O'- and 'A'-level GCE subjects, and a variety of external degrees under a service originally named the 'Open University'. The demolition of its Gothic mansion had meant it had to find new accommodation which it did in the form of a shed in Shaftesbury Road leased from the Cambridge University Press in September 1964.[20] To this was added the pre-fabricated former dining hall of Churchill College, whose Master, the Nobel laureate Sir John Cockroft, formally opened it on 4 June 1965, noting in his speech an occasion of its former use by the NEC for a residential course in economics.[21]

Much more importantly, Brian had to find staff for the rapidly expanding college and in particular an executive director to run its day-to-day affairs. Hilary Perraton succeeded David Grugeon as Administrator in 1964 but then became the college's first Educational Director the following year. John Griffiths seems to have been the first to hold the post of Executive Director but left it towards the end of 1966. Emmeline Garnett, who had a background in both education and broadcasting, had written scripts for the earliest joint BBC/NEC series, *After School English*, was approached.[22] Brian appears to have wanted her to take charge after John Griffiths left – he was preparing to set up an NEC scheme for Industrial Training and, subject to funding by the British Government, a branch of the NEC in Ghana – but she was tied up elsewhere.[23] In the event Brian had to use the firm of John Tyzac and Partners to recruit a replacement. His brief proposed someone who 'must be a graduate but preferably with administrative experience in industry rather than education'. D.W.B. (David) Baron, an ex-senior colonial administrator with experience in Hong Kong was the person chosen to take charge of the college which then had a staff of thirty and an annual turnover of more than £50,000.[24] David Baron then appointed Alan Charnley to replace Hilary Perraton as Educational Director in July 1967, a post he held until the crisis of 1971.[25]

In the meantime events were beginning to move towards the establishment of the Open University. Harold Wilson, by then Prime Minister of his second Labour Government, announced that Jenny Lee, Minister of State for the Arts, was to take responsibility for its creation. The first time she had heard about the proposal, as she recalled later, was when he said to her in the summer of 1965, 'For God's sake try to get this thing going! The department of Education and Science is the most reactionary department in the Government; I can get no help either from the senior officials or the Ministers.'[26] Brian Jackson was on to it immediately. He wrote a long piece in the *Guardian*, 22 June 1965, which began 'Jenny Lee . . . is now settling down to hammer out the practical details of a University of the Air. It is a relief to those of us who have helped to pilot this project that action is imminent; . . .' and he went on to summarise his experiences to date, stressing the importance of television – 'perhaps the sole basis' – and describing in detail the experimental courses in English and maths which the NEC ran in conjunction with Anglia Television. These incorporated the concept of the correspondence courses being written by the television tutors and backed up by residential schools at Clare College, Cambridge. As he then wrote: 'It was, I believe, the first time in the world that the three teaching techniques – broadcasts, correspondence, residence – had been quite so closely fused.'[27] The article went on to outline various problems likely to face the new university including how best to correlate broadcasting with correspondence work, the advantages of radio for certain subjects, who the students were likely to be and how many of them would want to take the opportunity offered. Throughout the piece he wrote as though he expected to play a significant part in the development of the Open University and in conclusion said; 'It is so easy with such a novel and publicly exciting project to forget its prime purpose. I am strongly in favour of research and caution lest the publicity run away with us. . . . I'd hate a fanfare of trumpets announcing a University of the Air which proves to have no claims to be a university at all, and which could, just conceivably, turn into the groundnuts fiasco of the present time.'

But Brian's vision of the new university was not to be. When Jenny Lee, by then Parliamentary Under-secretary at the Department of Education and Science, scrapped the department's plans which despite Harold Wilson's animadversions seem to have been prepared in some detail, she failed to include Brian Jackson in the eclectic Advisory Committee which she assembled and, apparently determined to maintain a firm grip on it, chaired herself.[28] Nevertheless Brian, on behalf of the NEC, continued to woo her. The White Paper entitled *A University of the Air* was published in February 1966. In October 1966 the *Cambridge Review* carried an article by Jenny Gunby, a New-Zealander, who was described as 'Special Projects Officer, National Extension College' entitled 'The Open University'. In it she described the plight of thousands of students taking London University degree courses solely by correspondence and their delight at being able to attend the experimental residential courses being run by the NEC under that title.[29] One of the students described the very course referred to by Sir John Cockroft as follows:

> I started this degree lark because I wanted to understand things . . . so I thought; right, Economics – that's the thing, and I've been bashing away at it by correspondence for a couple of years now. But this week is the first time I've ever had the chance to talk to a real economist. Never seen one before! I just can't describe what a chance like that means.

Jenny Gunby went on to give further details and claimed the college was ready to expand the scheme.[30] The Minister was invited to visit the NEC and did so informally that same autumn. On 29 September 1966 she wrote to Brian, 'I have seen with interest the National Extension College's plans for . . . external students. May I congratulate you on your initiative. . . . I am hoping that we shall be in a position to make a public statement about the Open University Project before long. With best wishes, Yours sincerely' (both hand written, as was 'Dear Brian Jackson').[31] In December 1966 she gave an interview to Jenny Gunby and this was published in the first edition of the NEC's students' magazine, *home study* (sic) in March 1967. The cover of the magazine showed Miss Lee talking to NEC students in Cambridge during her visit. In the interview the term Open University, signifying that no entrance qualifications would be required, was used throughout as the title of the projected institution but the Minister continued to maintain, however politely, her distance. The same quiet refusal to be drawn was maintained in further correspondence between Brian and the Minister and a reply to Brian signed by her private secretary, Michael James, in November 1967 thanked him for the NEC Progress Report and suggested that he might like to send a copy to the Open University Planning Committee at Richmond Terrace, Whitehall.[32]

Meanwhile developments were occurring on several other fronts. The NEC was getting its act together as a correspondence college and expanding: by March 1967 it was catering for 7,000 students served by some 350 teachers.[33] In May 1966, still assuming the NEC would have a major role to play in the recently announced Open University, Brian launched a scheme to buy Cheshunt College and use it as an Open College to provide combined residential and tutorial facilities. Cheshunt had been founded in South Wales in 1768 by that redoubtable reformer, Selina, Countess of Huntingdon and used latterly to train Congregationalist ministers. Selina's descendant, the current countess, Margaret Lane, together with Michael Young, Brian Jackson, and John Scupham OBE, the former head of BBC Education, all spoke at a press conference on 19 December 1966 at the Waldorf Hotel, Aldwych to launch an appeal for funds. The NEC proposed renting the college but this scheme was not accepted and offers to purchase were invited by 31 December 1966. An Open College Progress report on 1 December 1966 was followed by a newsletter on 30 March 1967 which referred to Peter Laslett seeking funds in the United States despite the deadline for offers having by then passed.[34] The Department of Education and Science were unhelpful. Brian described them even more scathingly than Harold Wilson had done as acting 'like the bow-tie'd pianist in the brothel' who simply didn't know what was going on in the other rooms.[35] Sufficient funds were not forthcoming and as Brian later wrote, 'apart from Sir Eric Ashby, Lord Annan, and Professor Sir Nevill Mott, the University held ranks'. The college was sold as a retirement home for Freemasons. Seven years later, no retired Freemasons having appeared, it was rented out as offices.[36]

Never one to be daunted by setbacks, Brian was banging on the door of the Open University planners in March 1968 with a proposal for the NEC to provide the correspondence content of its courses. A covering letter to the chairman, Sir Peter Venables, outlined their case briefly, which was: they had experience of students and of co-operation with the BBC and also contacts with several universities and local education authorities whose premises they had used out of term time. In short, they had pioneered all the techniques the OU was proposing to adopt. On 26 February 1968 Brian sent out letters outlining these proposals to a wide variety of people hoping to lobby the NEC's case before attending a meeting with the Planning Committee at 38 Belgrave Square. The minutes, written up by David Baron who was also present at the meeting on 25 March 1968, noted that 'The meeting ended without specific conclusion or agreement or further action'. Subsequently a letter from D.V. Stafford, Secretary to the Planning Committee to Brian Jackson, referring to the same meeting confirmed that 'The delegation on the lines proposed would be incompatible with the proper exercise of the University's responsibilities under its charter'.[37] So that was finally that. There was, however, a tiny consolation prize. The Committee issued a press release, dated 7 March 1968, about its proposed curriculum which said it did not intend to run preparatory courses but 'other agencies will be invited and encouraged to co-operate in making this provision'.[38]

Looking back at 1967, the year in which the NEC made its first small surplus, Brian Jackson wrote, 'Despite our vast and complex educational system there is still room for enterprise and self-help, when it is clear that Government or Local Authorities cannot act. . . .' but by June 1968 David Baron, in his report to the college's newly-acquired board of Trustees was sounding a less optimistic note:

> A progress report on an educational venture should not start with finance, which should properly be the servant of NEC's aims; but in practice finance has tended to be largely the master – not a flexible framework but a straitjacket. The overriding necessity to increase

cash inflow, if NEC was not to founder, and to stave off NEC obli-
gations by every possible device in order to reduce cash outflow,
has coloured and even distorted our programme. The treasurer has
steered with great skill to keep NEC afloat.[39]

The college appears to have shared its treasurer with ACE, for in April
1968 Baron wrote to Conrad Halloran – whom Brian had appointed to replace
Howard Dickinson in January 1965 – 'how grateful I am for your constant
support . . . steered our finances most skilfully in rough seas. . .'.[40] The
background to this state of affairs was that the Gulbenkian grants had ended
in 1965 whilst the windfall from the UCC had been spent on refurbishing the
course materials, leaving the college almost entirely dependent on income
from student fees. Apart from the fluctuation in this source – most of the fee
money came in September or January – there were too few students to cover
the standing costs. The College needed 10,000, but had only 7,000, and its
fees, moreover, were still uncompetitive compared to those of the traditional
commercial colleges.[41] Thus, despite the bitter disappointment at being totally
bypassed by the Open University Planning Committee when they had
reasonably hoped for a major role in its foundation, the offer to produce the
correspondence side of a series of preparatory courses was most welcome.
These were to be sponsored by the OU and organised by the BBC, using
methods that the OU was proposing to use itself. The work came as a life-
saver. Though it was not prepared to recognise these courses officially as a
'gateway' to the new university – one of its key premises was that no formal
entry qualifications were required – the Open University helped pay for the
development costs and publicity for the courses, and in addition financed a
research project to assess their impact.

Naomi McIntosh (Sargeant), who later became a Trustee of the NEC, was
the Open University's Research Officer in charge of the project which sought
to establish the sorts of applicants the OU might expect to get by sending
out questionnaires with the Gateway material. Her report, *An Integrated
Multi-Media Educational Experience. . ?,* was produced in July 1970. But
Brian Jackson was also very interested in this question. He reported in the
Sunday Times, 25 November 1969, that the Open University was in danger of
attracting the wrong students. Of the first two hundred to enrol for the
Gateway courses seventy-six per cent had stayed at school beyond the age
of sixteen, while no less than ninety per cent had some GCEs. Was this sour
grapes? Possibly, but an independent article by Lewis Chester, also in the
Sunday Times, to coincide with the first intake of students in January 1971
asked 'Has It Lost Its Way?' and pointed out that Brian Jackson's proposal
of an Open University in *Education and the Working Class* – 'the earliest
reference anyone can recall' – said such a university would entail 'a large
new working-class intake', and that although Jenny Lee supported this, in
the event 'the first intake had included 33.6 per cent teachers, 11.3 per cent

from the professions and the arts, and 8.9 per cent housewives. . . .'[42]

Whilst the work instigated by the Open University provided a very useful contribution to the NEC's finances – over a third of its turnover in the year to 1970 – the problems of funding continued to be a worry. The trustees decided to approach the Department of Education and Science for a grant and possibly to this end decided, despite the Department's earlier affirmation that such a thing was impossible, to commission an independent inspection by John Blackie, CBE, MA, formerly HM Government's Chief Inspector of Primary Schools. Just how independent this was is open to doubt, since Brian wrote to Eric Midwinter on another occasion 'you'll like him [John Blackie], I did, even when he inspected me as a primary-school teacher'.[43] Blackie's report was, in the event, though sympathetic, both balanced and constructively critical, praising especially the morale of the staff, 'At present at least four of [them] whose work could be most efficiently carried out in private rooms are obliged to occupy desks in the open office. That they do so cheerfully, or at least uncomplainingly, is a tribute to the dedication they bring to their work. . . .'[44] The report was dated 24 December 1969. David Baron, admittedly not a man to be parsimonious with compliments but nevertheless expressing sentiments similar to those expressed by others of Brian's ex-colleagues, wrote to Brian immediately following the report with fulsome praise for 'your wise counsel . . . not fully appreciated by Michael or anyone else to what extent I have relied on your intuition, resource – and optimism – to see NEC through . . . the direction at critical moments owes far more to you than to me. . . . I am immensely grateful for all that you have done to sustain me in the past and to keep NEC afloat. . .'.[45] But matters did not improve. In May 1970 Conrad Halloran was forced to go cap-in-hand to the Open University explaining that they had spent the six-months grant for Gateway research in four months 'due to not having allowed for some £450 postage and £100 stationery' and asked for a further £1,500 'preferably before the May salaries fall due'.[46] Some of the deficit may have been caused by more than failure to 'allow for' as the case of a Mr Gupta may show. He was, sentenced to three years at Cambridge Crown Court in 1973 for having embezzled £9,568.64 from the NEC stamp money and 'having transferred the proceeds of the sale of his houses to India' was unable to refund the monies.[47]

Indeed, things financial seem to have gone from bad to worse for the NEC during 1970. The budget for 1971 was reduced by about a third mainly due, as Brian wrote in a subsequent report, 'to the BBC becoming alarmed at the college's dependence on it' with the result that the income from the Gateway courses was dropped from £53,000 to £10,000.[48] The imminent coming on-stream of the Open University left a question mark hanging over the continuing viability of the NEC which cannot have helped morale. In efforts to diversify and find new roles further time and energy were dissipated: for example in preparing an economics course in conjunction with Manchester

University which had not, as yet, shown dividends. Then the worst that could happen to a correspondence college happened: a postal strike occurred. In January 1971 Tom Jackson, the genial and famously-moustachioed general secretary of their union, had brought the postal workers out on strike. As a final blow Cambridge University Press called in the lease and the college was forced to move in with ACE, who fortunately by then were established in Fitzwilliam House.[49]

Not surprisingly, the college collapsed. After making Alan Charnley redundant, and writing him a glowing testimonial, David Baron himself resigned in April 1971. Brian was forced to step in and take control. Richard Blake became executive director of both ACE and NEC, at no extra salary, there were no funds.[50] In a memo to the Chairman of the trustees, Sir Nevill Mott, Master of Gonville and Caius College, Brian reported that the collapse 'was unnecessary. Pressures were considerable, but what caused it was panic among the senior staff – a desire to be free of "frontier post" responsibilities, and back in more secure roles.'[51] In addition to poor morale and lack of space, Brian discovered that the college had other problems. Several of the courses were faulty and there was no system for assessing or updating them.

> David left all 'educational' matters to Alan . . . [who] appears to
> have spread confusion all around him. It was difficult to get good
> handover information [about the Manchester Economics Project,
> which] . . . appears to have been tackled in a very higgledy-piggledy
> way. Again this produced avoidance reactions, and a temptation to
> call it all off. But in fact the project materials [a dozen or so books,
> films, correspondence course] will all be ready some time in 1972.
> Richard will pick up the threads, and at some point the finished
> package should join the Nuffield Science package as part of our
> Educational Resources Unit.[52]

Brian went on to describe steps taken by Richard and himself to put the NEC back on its feet. By far the most important was when a delegation consisting of Brian and the Trustees, led by the Chairman, Sir Nevill Mott, approached the Secretary of Education and Science – Margaret Thatcher – for a grant. According to Michael Young it was Brian who did all the talking.[53] His approach was effective and Mrs Thatcher bailed him out with £25,000.

Brian had gone in prepared. The report continues; 'Fly in our ointment turned out to be our non-joining of the Accreditation Council. Forewarned by Lord Boyle, we were able to invite the Accreditation Council people up to lunch with the chairman – before he met the Minister. The second year's grant seems assured; joining the Accreditation Council is necessary in 1972; and a press conference with Mrs Thatcher might open the way to discussions on the longer-term grant.'[54] This was a necessary climb-down on Brian's part as the NEC's proposal for an independant Accreditation Council, on the grounds that the existing one was not rigorous enough, had been refused .[55]

It would seem that Edward Boyle was sympathetic to the NEC and that, when he needed them, Brian had friends in high places. Moreover he clearly put himself and the NEC over to the Minister, with some justification despite his lifelong avowal of socialism, as prime exponents of Samuel Smiles-style self-help. It was a fitting end to Brian's struggles on its behalf, and for the NEC a new beginning, from which it has never looked back.

The memo stretches to seventeen pages. It shows clearly that Richard Blake was responsible for the day-to-day work of putting the pieces back together under Brian's general direction and outlines their plans for re-establishing the NEC, many of which came to fruition. One that did not was Brian's recommendation to Sir Nevill to appoint Richard Blake Director of NEC. Richard was unaware of this but confirms that he and his wife were duly 'given the full works' by Sir Nevill – dinner at High Table and all – but he declined the offer. He felt there was more excitement and a greater challenge, at that time, at ACE which he recalls, despite all the hard work, as 'undoubtedly the happiest years' of his working life. Brian, he said, 'empowered you'.[56]

As with ACE, Brian Jackson had created the NEC and built it into a large and successful national organisation in less than ten years. In addition he had seen it through considerable troubles and secured its financial future. Although it did not develop, as Brian had hoped it would, into the OU, it continued to grow and is still a flourishing and highly regarded institution.

Notes

1. Harold Wilson, 'In the Beginning', *The First Ten Years – A Special Edition of Sesame* (1979) p.2.
2. *The Times,* 25 May 1995, p.25.
3. Brian Jackson, 'The Invisible College' *The First Ten Years – A Special Edition of Sesame* (1979) p.24.
4. Harry Ree, foreword to 1986 edition of *Education and the Working Class.*
5. Brian Jackson, 'The Invisible College'.
6. Michael Young, 'A tribute to Brian Jackson' *Where?* 191 (September 1983).
7. Actually the meeting in Cambridge was in 1962 when Young was appointed to teach at the University and Brian Jackson took over the almost defunct Advisory Centre for Education. This in turn spawned the National Extension College in 1963 when the events Young describes did indeed take place.
8. Peter Laslett 'Tribute to Brian Jackson' *Where?* 95 (August 1974).
9. Letter to Kit Hardwick from Shirley Williams, 15 November 1996.
10. *The National Extension College*, p.2.
11. Letter from David Grugeon to Brian Jackson, 22 October 1964, F11.
12. Draft application by Brian Jackson, 7 November 1963, F11.
13. Brian Jackson 'Dawn University', *Where?* 17 (Summer 1964).
14. *The National Extension College.*
15. Transcript of a conference speech by Anthony Crosland, Douglas, April 1965, C5.

16. Letter Edward Short to Brian Jackson, NEC, 14 August 1968, F3.
17. Janet Jenkins and Hilary Perraton *The Invisible College: NEC 1963-1979*, p.22.
18. *idem.*
19. *ibid.*, p.23.
20. *The National Extension College*, p.6.
21. Correspondence Sir John Cockroft, Brian Jackson. Transcript of speech of Sir John. F12.
22. *The Invisible College*, p.15.
23. Letter from Brian Jackson to Emmeline Garnet, 7 December 1966.
24. Correspondence, Brian Jackson and John Tyzac and Partners. Letter of appointment, 14 January 1967, F11.
25. Letter of appointment, 4 May 1967, F11.
26. Jenny Lee in *The First Ten Years*, p.4.
27. Brian Jackson, 'University of the Air', *Guardian*, 22 June 1965, p.9.
28. *The First Ten Years*, p.5.
29. Jenny Gunby 'The Open University', *Cambridge Review* 15 October 1966 pp.21-23.
30. *idem.*
31. Letter Jenny Lee to Brian Jackson, 29 September 1966, F7.
32. Letter from Michael James to Brian Jackson, 3 November 1967, F1.
33. Brian Jackson, leader in *home study* No.1 (March 1967).
34. File on Cheshunt College, F12.
35. MS of Article, F8.
36. Memo by Brian Jackson F10.
37. Letter from D.V. Stafford, 16 May 1968, F7.
38. Proposal for the Open University to work through the NEC on the correspondence side, 14 March 1968, F7.
39. David Baron quoted in *The National Extension College*, p.8.
40. Letter to Conrad Halloran, 30 April 1968, F11.
41. *The National Extension College*, p.8.
42. Press cuttings, *Sunday Times*, 25 November 1969 and 3 January 1971, F7.
43. Letter to Eric Midwinter, 18 May 1971, C9.
44. Quoted in *The National Extension College*, p.9.
45. Handwritten letter from David Baron, 25 January 1970, F8.
46. Letter, Conrad Halloran to J.H. Austin, Finance Officer, Open University, Walton Hall, Bletchley, 1 May 1970, F8.
47. Report of case, 13 July 1973, and correspondence with Messrs Spicer and Pegler, Auditors, F10.
48. Revised Budget for 1971, 6 May 1971, F10. Report to Gulbenkian Foundation by Brian Jackson, Acting Director, NEC, March 1972, F10.
49. *The National Extension College*, p.9.
50. Interview with Richard Blake, 23 September 1994.
51. Report by Brian Jackson to Sir Nevill Mott, January 1972, F10.
52. PC of memo, hand-written, Brian Jackson to Sir Nevill Mott, about 'what directing NEC from April to December 1971 has meant. . . .', F10.
53. Interview with Michael Young, 24 September 1993.
54. PC of memo, as above.
55. Letter from Edward Short to Brian Jackson, NEC, 14 August 1968, F3.
56. Interview with Richard Blake, 23 September 1994.

Chapter 4
Power to the People

'The best argument for comprehensive schools', as Melvyn Bragg once memorably suggested 'is that if people do not know what might be available they are unlikely to ask for it.'[1] As Jackson and Marsden showed, many working-class children and their parents were woefully ignorant about educational possibilities.[2] Telling people what was available was the whole purpose of the Advisory Centre for Education and yet the people most in need of information, those parents so graphically identified in *Education and the Working Class,* were still not being reached. ACE's service rarely filtered beyond the articulate middle classes. The Education Shop and the various schemes it subsequently spawned, including the experiments at Butlin's holiday camps of the early 1970s were Brian's attempts to overcome this. The purpose of this chapter is to explore the different ways in which Brian Jackson tried to spread the necessary information more widely. Brian was nothing if not an opportunist, and he never missed any chance to put his ideas into practice on behalf of any group he perceived to be in some way underprivileged, or to further publicise ACE, especially if his practical interventions could be funded by some relevant charity. The routine day-by-day business of ACE, once he had got it up and running, never seems to have provided enough excitement for his mercurial personality.

'The Education Shop,' wrote Brian, 'was a pilot experiment'.[3] The idea was to persuade local authorities to spend more time helping parents who needed help. 'It was a symbolic project designed to change the atmosphere, to arouse discussion, and at the very least to awaken some of the more lethargic authorities into hostility.'[4] To attract the sort of parents who would not normally write to ACE and might be diffident about authority the shop needed to be easy to find, set in familiar surroundings, and staffed by easily approachable people who lacked any aura of officialdom. An obvious choice was a shopping centre. The head of the education department of Ipswich co-operative society, Alderman Dick Lewis, read about ACE's plans in the *Sunday Times* and arranged an offer of floor space in the Co-op's main town-centre department store. It was opened by Sir John Newsom on 15 October 1965 and ran until the following Saturday 23 October 1965.

Leaflets announcing the shop were sent to schools to be handed out to children and further publicity was gained through posters, newspapers and TV. The shop consisted of a small exhibition of general information on education and a counter staffed by two or three advisers from ACE. It attracted 225 visitors and it was felt that more might have come if the crowd at busy times had not frightened some less confident questioners away. Two-fifths of the questions came from manual and clerical and shop workers – a class that hardly figured at all in the membership of ACE – although the majority did come from traditional sources. 'Almost half of the lower middle and working classes said they had been just passing by, and taken the opportunity offered to ask their question.'[5] The questions dwelt primarily on careers and further education, then on schools. Next came problems connected with school work and, far behind, health and behaviour problems. There were few complaints and, by and large, the middle classes sought more specific, and the working classes more general, advice. Lindsey March, who monitored and wrote up the experiment, concluded that the shop's main faults were due to its small size. 'It was hard to find and it lacked privacy.'[6] But all in all the advisers considered the enthusiasm and interest shown by the visitors indicated that a need existed. Furthermore the demonstration did encourage other experiments.

In Manchester, Leonard Cohen, who was a member of the Education Committee and a reader of *Where?*, also happened to be chairman of Henry's, a large and rather down-market department store. The committee ran a shop there for a week which then transferred for a second week to the Co-op in Wythenshawe, the huge council estate south of the city. These were organised by Christopher Moor, the newly-appointed educational advisory officer for the city, and they attracted a similar number of visitors as the Ipswich shop but, though there was no follow-up research, it seemed likely from their location that they had reached a more working-class audience. Frank Pedley, who later became vice-chairman of the council of ACE, was chief education officer of Wigan and two shops were run briefly in stores there in 1968. Other experimental shops were run in Basildon, where the chief education officer, Mr E.A.Dixon, took part informally, and Brighton, where Dick Freeman of the ACE Advisory Service went down to help. The chief education officer of Essex, David Bungey, who read about the experiment later set up a more permanent scheme where senior members of his staff were available at various branch libraries throughout the county on a regular basis four times a year.

Sadly the report of the experiments described above, which was published by ACE in 1970, showed that the idea had never really got off the ground.[7] A large fascia sign in Oldham town centre in 1994 proclaiming the Education Shop revealed nothing more than the office where student grants and free school meals were dealt with and whose counter staff had never heard of Brian Jackson, let alone the Ipswich experiment.[8] Still, whoever named it may have subconsciously remembered those distant days at Henry's or Wythenshawe Co-op.

Yet another attempt to reach a large working-class audience was launched in the summer of 1972 when a team from ACE, led by Richard Blake and Barrie Knight, set up shop at Butlin's Holiday Camp at Pwllheli. Richard Blake as executive director of ACE had the job of approaching Butlin's management for permission and financial assistance, both of which were granted. He tells the story of being ushered into the inner sanctum at the London head-quarters and, when asked if he had noticed anything unusual about the desk, saw that it was embellished with swastikas. It transpired that upon hearing war declared in 1939 Billy Butlin had immediately spotted that the German Embassy would have no further use for its fine furniture which could thus be acquired at a knock-down price.[9] It was perhaps this memory that prompted Richard and Barrie to send a telegram to ACE announcing their safe arrival at Pwllheli and that they had already begun to tunnel their way out.[10] The experiment went well and it was expanded in the following year to include four weeks at the camp at Clacton in Essex and six weeks at Pwllheli and large numbers of staff, as well as sympathetic outside recruits who were associated with both ACE and NEC projects, did turns of duty. The internal report shows that most of the middle-class altruists who staffed the shops absolutely hated it. Brian himself said during the course of a lecture he gave some years later in Sheffield, 'Butlin's is a shocking place to live in, but people on holiday there, in a grim way, thought of it as paradise.'[11] Such insights provide an ironic commentary on the whole ACE ethos and particularly on Brian's claim to revere the special values of working-class culture, yet, with the mellowing of time and distance, most have very fond memories of their time at Butlin's.[12] At least two marriages of ACE's volunteers had their germination during the experiment. Barrie Knight, as ACE's Director of the Community Education Project, held a meeting in October 1973 to decide whether to approach Butlin's for finance to run the scheme in all its camps for the whole of the following summer, or at least for the school holidays, or whether to abandon the idea. He took along the reports of five of the previous summer's team leaders. One reckoned that the operation had been under-resourced both in money and people and that three weeks was long enough to ask anyone to lead a team. A second leader though much time had been wasted answering similar questions over and over again and that a more formal structure with lectures on selected topics such as 'How to start a playgroup', or 'What to do if the head doesn't want parents' (sic) would have been more useful. He would not personally be prepared to do more than one week in any future scheme. A third, who noted confusion about aims and conflict with Butlin's staff, said it was 'bloody hard graft, not a holiday' and that the expenses were ludicrous: 'If anyone wasn't out of pocket he's either a misanthrope or a tee-totaller – or both!' He was sufficiently disenchanted with the experience to avow that in any future venture two weeks would be the maximum he could stand. Two others agreed that a fortnight was enough and one of these would only do it if wives were allowed and self-catering chalets provided.[13] John Pollit who was at Pwllheli sounds to have tried to enjoy the experience despite never quite knowing 'who was supposed to be doing what' and having reservations about the arrangements for payment, but even he reported ruefully that a disastrous fire had destroyed much paperwork. As a result the four weeks at Clacton produced 131 recorded interviews and Pwllheli's six weeks only 125 from a total of 774 and 799 initial contacts respectively. Contacts with the children appear to have been more plentiful: the file on Butlin's in the archives contains masses of children's competition work as witness to this.

The experiment was, nevertheless, extended for a further year when teams opened up shop at Butlin's camps at Filey and Skegness. In all, over seventy people, teachers, social workers, friends and associates of ACE and the NEC, took part over the three years but no further expansion ensued as the scheme was one of several which were scrapped by John Hipkin as part of his retrenchment when he took over from Brian as director of ACE in July 1974.[14] The three years had, however, been a useful, if salutary, experience and they led to some significant developments. One of those recruited in 1974 was Sandra Last, a former ACE typist, who subsequently rejoined Brian as secretary of the national Educational Research and Development Trust, NERDT, and later became his personal secretary, aid, and amanuensis right up to the time of his death.[15] Another of the outside participants who was at Butlin's that year was Trevor Burgin, a former Huddersfield headmaster who became Advisor for Multi-Cultural Education in the Kirklees Education Department and was later honoured for his pioneering work teaching English to Asian children. It was he who, hearing from Brian that he was currently looking for someone to organise a new project for childminders in Huddersfield, introduced him to a member of his staff: Hazel Wigmore.[16] Hazel was subsequently seconded to NERDT in the autumn of 1974 and the following year, financed initially by a grant from the Wates Foundation, employed by the Trust as Director of the National Children's Centre in Huddersfield, the post she held until 2001.

A somewhat different opportunity to take information directly to the people presented itself in the autumn of 1972 when General Idi Amin announced in August that all British Asians in Uganda had to leave the country by 8 November 1972. Some 27,000 of these refugees arrived in the United Kingdom and many were temporarily housed in camps, though by early December less than 10,000 remained there, and most of these were re-housed within twelve months. Douglas Tilbe, a friend of Brian's from the AMP and Birmingham Playgroup days was chairman of the Co-ordinating Committee for the Welfare of Evacuees from Uganda, CCWEU, and ACE quickly sent teams to the camps to offer advice on educational matters. Information on what was required was gleaned from the first immigrants at Stradishall Camp near London and leaflets were duly prepared. Julia McGawley had these translated into Gugurati and printed whilst Brian, who was based at the Midland Hotel in Manchester at the time, wrote to the Press to publicise the needs of the refugees (26 September 1972) and on 29 September 1972 to confirm plans for a camp education shop with Douglas Tilbe and to drum up the funds for it. Mr Pratap Chitnis of the Joseph Rowntree Social Service Trust in York responded positively and quickly on 6 October 1972 to an initial request for £1,000 and by early November he provided a further £3,000 for various schemes including a mobile education shop and a playgroup bus for Tonfanau Camp in Merionethshire.[17] Anne Garvey took the playbus and her penetrating report of the problems and conditions at Tonfanau – 'possibly the coldest place on Earth, a sort of Welsh Gulag' – evokes the pattern of the whole settlement exercise in microcosm.[18] The caterers made no attempt to provide food suitable for Asian vegetarians – egg and chips, served three times on one memorable day, was the closest they got – while the Government's efforts to disperse the refugees – as far afield as to Wick in Caithness in one case – were strongly resisted by the people themselves who wanted to join already-established Asian communities in such places as Leicester or Manchester. Anne also wrote about the conditions in a letter to the *Guardian* and apparently gained some good publicity for ACE's cause. She subsequently got a job with the advisory service and later worked closely with Brian on the problems of Chinese children in Britain.[19]

Meanwhile Brian discovered that there were numbers of qualified teachers among the immigrants who were bilingual in English and Gugurati but whose qualifications were not recognised in this country. He campaigned long and hard, though ultimately fruitlessly, for at least temporary recognition of their qualifications. On 3 October 1972 he wrote to ask if Mrs Thatcher could help. She replied on 30 October that she regretted she could not, but hinted at a possible loophole; that local Education Authorities could employ unqualified staff at their own discretion subject to her department's approval. Brian also wrote on 3 October 1972 to the General Secretary of the National Union of Teachers, Mr Edward Britton, asking if the immigrant teachers could be given even a temporary licence to teach, especially since so many of the Asian children would eventually be settling in Educational Priority Areas where there were already problems enough, not least a shortage of bilingual teaching staff. Maurice Newrick, Assistant Secretary of the Education Committee of the NUT replied on 17 November 1972 that although the committee had 'great sympathy . . . [they) did not feel, however, that it would be consistent with the long-standing Union policy to raise the standards of qualification of the teaching profession, to propose any relaxation of the present rules governing recognition as a qualified teacher.'[20] It was small wonder that Brian had such a generally low opinion of teachers whom he saw as conservative forces opposed to change, as evidenced many years later in an interview with John Izbiki, education correspondent of the *Daily*

Telegraph. When referring to the desirability of adding Education for Parenthood to the curriculum he said; 'We must help create decent families before we can have a decent world. Perhaps now that the teacher-dominated Schools Council is to be axed, this will be easier to achieve.'[21]

Within twelve months most of these Ugandan Asians had left the camps and were settled for the most part, despite the efforts of the authorities, in the cities with existing major immigrant communities. As we now know from the numbers of Asian-owned paper shops and general food stores, many have prospered. Perhaps it does not matter therefore that Brian's efforts, culminating in a press release 18 September 1974 urging the new government to set up INN, an Institute for the Needs of Newcomers, using Common Market funds and based on the lessons learned over the previous two years with the Ugandan immigrants, came to nothing.[22]

An area where ACE became directly, and much more successfully, involved with working-class children and their parents was in the Liverpool Priority project. Brian's proposal to discriminate positively in the education of children whose family background and social environment were educationally handicapping was, as already noted, taken up by Plowden through the lobbying of Michael Young. As a result, five inner-city areas in London, Birmingham, Liverpool, the West Riding, and a Scottish one in Dundee were designated as Educational Priority Areas and the government made up to £100,000 available through the Department of Education and Science for a three-year programme. A further £75,000 was provided through the Social Science Research Council, of which Michael Young was chairman, as the experiment, in addition to positively discriminating 'to make schools in the most deprived areas as good as the best in the country', was also exhorted by Plowden, 'to discover which of the developments in the educational priority areas have the most constructive effects so as to assist in planning the longer-term programme'.[23] This was to be, in the words of its director Professor Halsey, 'a pioneering effort in the use of the action-research method in this country.'[24] Anthony Crosland, who left the DES in the Autumn of 1967, is on record as saying that the 'one major thing we had already done', in relation to processing the Plowden recommendations was 'to get the principle of educational priority areas accepted and to get an extra £16 million for them. It was almost the last thing I did at education and one of the things that gave me most satisfaction.'[25]

Of the five areas selected the Liverpool project, directed by Eric Midwinter, who came from Edge Hill College of Education in Liverpool and took up his new post in September 1968, was 'action dominated from the start'.[26] It was this project which Richard Blake, as Executive Director of ACE, visited in 1970. He was so impressed by the achievements of Midwinter and his team both in their efforts to promote pre-school education and their success in involving the local community that he urged Brian to go and see for himself, which he subsequently did.[27] One highly visible method used to help pre-school children was the 'Playbus' – a converted Liverpool Corporation Transport double-decker – which was inspired, according to Eric Midwinter, by 'The precedent of Mahomet and the mountain'.[28] Their success at involving the local community began by persuading local shops to display examples of children's work. Despite initial scepticism three shops agreed and a fish 'sculpted' from junk with a motor-cycle petrol tank for its body and bicycle bells for eyes was an instant hit in the local fishmongers, prompting a huge demand for photographs of it and a steady stream of visitors, many not even wanting to buy fish. This led to a major exhibition of school work at one of the city's largest department stores, 'Teejays' (T.J. Hughes) for two weeks in March 1970.[29] Was this a shade of the Ipswich Education Shop perhaps?

Certainly when Brian visited Eric Midwinter the two men hit it off instantly. Both dynamic 'do-ers' as well as being imaginative and creative thinkers, their beliefs and ideas about politics and education were very much in harmony. In addition they discovered they shared a northern working-class background and a love of football. They had been contemporaries at St Catharine's College, Cambridge but had not previously met.[30] As a result they proposed to find a way to continue the Liverpool EPA project after the government's three-year funding ran out.

Brian wrote to Eric Midwinter on 29 October 1970 and, referring to 'discussions in Liverpool last week', proposed a national organisation based on the Liverpool project to start in January 1972. He suggested that Midwinter should join ACE as a director and that two of his Liverpool committee should join the council of ACE. Furthermore he proposed to put the ACE Birmingham project under Eric's overall control. After spending a week in Cambridge, Eric Midwinter wrote Brian a long and enthusiastic letter, full of ideas for the new project, on 8 January 1971. This was followed by correspondence with the relevant people at ACE.[31] There was then a three-month gap in the correspondence which was doubtless caused by Brian's preoccupation elsewhere – the postal strike which almost scuppered the NEC occurred at this time – but on 7 April 1971 Brian wrote to report on his efforts to fund the new project: 'no luck with Leverhulme'. Then 28 April 1971 saw Brian writing about the re-structuring at ACE caused by the near-collapse of NEC and on the following day a further progress report on a lunch he and Richard (Blake) had with Lady Plowden who agreed to help in approaching an industrialist for funds and also promised to put their case to Mrs Thatcher who, at the Department of Education and Science, had just so marvellously bailed out the NEC. In May, Eric Midwinter replying to 'a sheaf of letters from you' reported he was to see John Moores 'this Friday' and indeed it was he who was eventually to play a major part in funding the whole operation and to become a member of ACE's governing body. The correspondence continued throughout the rest of that summer and into the autumn with all manner of ideas for seeking grants and generating income, such as from publishing or by linking 'Priority' with the government's adult education schemes. In this latter venture Brian enlisted the help of John Blackie, formerly Her Majesty's Chief Inspector of Primary Schools, The money must have been forthcoming as a formal offer of a job as co-director of ACE, in a triumvirate along with Brian and Richard Blake, was made to Eric Midwinter 15 July 1971.[32] In November, Michael Young agreed to Brian's proposal to invite John Moores onto their council and by January 1972 Eric Midwinter was writing on 'Priority' headed note paper datelined Harrison Jones CP School, Liverpool 7. Nevertheless Brian was still writing to the Van Leer Foundation, among other potential sources of funds, inviting them to attend the official announcement by ACE of the creation of 'Priority' on 26 January 1972.

During the following two years 'Priority' under Eric Midwinter's direction and with the assistance of some former EPA colleagues carried on the work begun under the government's scheme and strove to publicise its results. After research and action, dissemination was, as Professor Halsey noted, the third necessary function. 'Both the successes and the failures of research need to be known by all L.E.A.s and schools. A private venture – 'Priority' – based in Liverpool but national in aspiration has evolved. . . . It has support from the Liverpool Corporation and deserves more from other public bodies.'[33] Indeed, Halsey himself in addition to giving 'Priority' this official *imprimatur*, continued to take an active interest in its progress. As Eric Midwinter described the proposed centre:

> [it] has a number of functions. It endeavours to maintain and extend the actual Liverpool Project as a demonstration of urban community schooling; it acts as a co-ordination information centre for like work on a national scale; it publishes a thrice-yearly journal *Priority News*, and various books, reports and occasional papers; it will continue to produce prototype kits and other materials; and to offer a training service to those who feel in need of its support; it will attempt to float innovations and research probes up and down the country; it will take into account a full spectrum of need, from pre-school to adult education and including industry, theatre and all other aspects of community life; it will attempt to involve the popular media, such as the press and television in community education; it will try, with its Speakers' Panels, by conferences, courses and other means, to build up an audience for urban community schooling; in general, it will aim at keeping alive an enlarged and profound concept of the EPA problem and a vigorous and positive portrayal of its resolution.

He continued,

> With great foresight and wisdom, the Liverpool LEA has kindly given us the material wherewithal and full encouragement to establish our

centre in its midst, and, of course, their assistance is indispensable. The Social and Administrative Studies Department at Oxford – the original national base for the EPA Project – the Advisory Centre for Education at Cambridge, the Liverpool Council of Social Services, the pick of Liverpool Colleges, Merseyside business interests, including splendid support from John Moores Junior, and several other individuals and agencies, have promised vital support.[34]

It was a manifesto of such all-encompassing breadth and describing such grandiose intentions as to be worthy of the pen of Brian himself. Yet this was not just a pipe dream. By May 1972 in the second of its occasional papers 'Priority' was announcing that: '[its] Speakers' Panel has notched up over 40 appearances in the first four months of the year, including six one-day conferences and with Priority's director, Eric Midwinter, speaking at the important North of England Education Conference on 'Disadvantage' at Leeds and the highly significant Encyclopaedia Brittanica Seminar on 'the Urban Child' at the Festival Hall. Priority also organised its first ever course – for local education officers at Edge Hill College on 'the EPA Projects and After' with A. H. Halsey and Lady Plowden taking valuable parts.' A charming illustration of John Moores' generosity occurred when, invited to one such conference as guest -of-honour, he discretely asked what he should pay for attending.[35]

Priority News also reported a 'pleasing start' with Australian and Dutch addresses on its mailing list and that 'Priority' had made a meaningful television breakthrough by giving assistance to Granada's 'highly popular and useful advice programme *This Is Your Right,* thus furthering the cause of parental involvement and influence in education. Significantly *Priority News* also carried a report of the official opening of the 'Priority' Centre by Councillor Bushnell, Vice-Chairman of Liverpool Education Committee, and drew attention to the Centre's major feature: a 'well-equipped and comfortable teachers' workshop'.[36] As Brian later reported this was one scheme that came full circle when two years later Eric Midwinter took over a 'new and huge in-service training programme for young Liverpool teachers, and will combine that with all the exciting down-town projects that 'Priority' has built up.' He continued, 'During his two years with ACE in which he poured his energies into our whole range of activities, Eric built up the 'Priority' team and project until the moment when the local authority was ready to take it over. And so it has done.'[37] This was a classic example of Brian's dictum that 'ACE's job was to do itself out of a job'. What had started with an idea flown up by ACE became accepted by government as an experiment, was then further developed by ACE, and eventually taken back by local government. But it was not by any means the end of Eric Midwinter's involvement with ACE or his association with Brian.

Why did some projects work while others failed? The attempt to take information to a wider audience than the readership of *Where?* was a nice idea and one can readily understand, in the light the main theme of *Education and the Working Class*, why Brian should have been so keen to do so. Nevertheless John Hipkin was probably right to decide that ACE simply had not the resources either of personnel or of finance to develop such a service on a national scale and that anything less was insufficient.[38] The attempt to help Ugandan Asians was well-intentioned but Brian's efforts to get their teaching qualifications recognised came up against the resistance of the teaching unions and before he could prevail the problem had melted away as the refugees made their own arrangements and left the camps. The 'Priority' project in Liverpool succeeded for a number of reasons. It had been established with government funding. It enjoyed popularity and support in the community including the financial backing of local benefactor John Moores. Perhaps most of all it worked because in Eric Midwinter it had a leader with ability and energy similar to Brian's and the two were socially compatible. Moreover Midwinter was well-known locally, had worked for the local authority, and was prepared to see the scheme through until the authority recognised the advantages of taking it over themselves.

Notes

1. *Start the Week,* BBC Radio 4, 28 November 1994
2. Jackson and Marsden, *Education and the Working Class,* passim.
3. Brian Jackson, Review of the Education Shop in *1960-1970 A Progress Report,* pp.15-26, p.16.
4. *ibid.,* p.15.
5. Lindsey March, *The Education Shop,* p.26. I have used this and Jackson, *1960-1970 A Progress Report* for much of what follows.
6. March, *The Education Shop.*
7. Jackson, *1960-1970 A Progress Report,* pp.15-26.
8. Answers to author's personal enquiries.
9. Interview with Richard Blake, 23 September 1994.
10. *idem.*
11. Brian Jackson, 'Why not an open college now?',Second Arthur Jones Memorial Lecture, Melbourne House, Sheffield, 26 June 1976, F6.
12. Conversations with Trevor Burgin, John Pollit, Eric Midwinter and others.
13. Report on Butlin's ASK ACE in 1973, F5.
14. Sue Cameron 'Uneasy peace after ACE probe' *The Times Educational Supplement,* 7 February 1975.
15. Interview with Sandra Last, 23 September 1994.
16. Interview with Trevor Burgin, 25 May 1994.
17. The Playbus was an idea pioneered by the Liverpool EPA Project which is described later.
18. Anne Garvey 'The Great Camp Disaster' B5.
19. Interview with Anne Garvey, 22 September 1994.
20. Correspondence, B5.
21. John Izbiki, 'When bright pupils suffer', *Daily Telegraph,* 10 May 1982, p.10.

22. Draft proposal to 'a few friends', by Brian Jackson, August 1973. Press release, Cambridge Educational and Development Trust, 18 September 1974, B5.
23. Quoted by A.H. Halsey, *Educational Priority Vol I*, p vii.
24. *ibid.*, p vii.
25. Anthony Crosland interviewed on 7 September 1970, in Maurice Kogan, *The Politics of Education*, p.197.
26. Halsey, *Educational Priority Vol I*, p ix.
27. Interview with Richard Blake, 23 September 1994.
28. Eric Midwinter, *Priority Education*, p.66.
29. *ibid.*, p.150.
30. Various correspondence and conversations with Eric Midwinter who has been most kind and helpful to me throughout my researches.
31. File of letters, C9.
32. *ibid.*
33. Halsey, *Educational Priority Vol I*, p.197.
34. Midwinter, *Priority Education*, pp.183-184.
35. Interview with Richard Blake, 23 September 1994.
36. *Priority News*, May 1972, p.12.
37. Brian Jackson, 'Adieu to two', *Where? 91*, April 1974.
38. Interview with John Hipkin, 15 October 1996.

Chapter 5
Brian Jackson and the Media: publicity and the spoken word

Brian Jackson had a natural affinity for publicity and used the media shamelessly throughout his life to plug the causes he believed in. From his earliest attempts to finance the trip he and his friends made to prospect for gold in Lapland to his untimely death taking part in a fun run round the streets of Huddersfield to raise money for the National Children's Centre, he was never far from the limelight. His form master's remarks in the report at the end of Brian's first term in the sixth form were: 'He has adapted himself very well to sixth-form work and is prominent in the debating society.[1] He was to remain prominent in a much broader debate for the next thirty-five years. Brian seems to have enjoyed publicity. He was, according to many of his friends, forceful and opinionated, which would have made him an ideal interviewee. But he does seem to have overestimated his abilities when he tried to set up his own radio station.[2] Not only did he fail, but he appears to have pursued the idea, against the odds, long after it should have been clear that it was not a viable proposition. The purpose of this chapter is to look at Brian Jackson's early broadcasting experience and to examine the saga of Radio Cambridge. Why was Brian so keen to create a commercial radio station with a cultural and educational output? Why did he badger away at it for so long and why ultimately did he fail?

His first appearance on TV seems to have been on Anglia's *Life is what you make it* on 17 August 1961, but it was the publication of *Education and the Working Class* the following February that first brought Brian to the attention of the media in a serious way.[3] He appeared with John Dekker on the North of England Home Service on 2 March 1962, for which he received five guineas plus fares, and the following day took part in *The World of Books* on the London Home Service for ten guineas.[4] On 21 March 1962 he was paid fifteen guineas for appearing in *Perspective: Class* on BBC TV but two days earlier with Anglia TV he earned twenty guineas for talking about the eleven-plus exam on *Look to Tomorrow*.[5] Throughout the rest of the year – which saw him take over the near-defunct Advisory Centre for Education during the summer – he appeared in a variety of programmes. In June he talked about *Education and the Working Class* on the North East Home Service and in August he took part in a programme entitled *Too Many Exams?* on the London Home Service and a BBC television programme called *In their Opinion*. By November 1962 he was appearing in a programme of his own on

Network Three entitled *Unread Classics: Little Dorrit* for which he was paid the handsome sum – for those days – of thirty guineas.[6] No wonder the transcript, on yellowing foolscap, is still in his archive.

During 1963 Brian took part in a number of discussions, both on radio and television, as Director of ACE. In January he spoke for three minutes about state versus private education on Network Three and about schools generally on a *Tonight* programme on television produced by Anthony Jay.[7] On 27 February 1963 he took part in *Table Talk*, a lunch-format discussion pro-gramme in which such diverse opinions as those of the (then) young Peregrine Worsthorne, Katharine Whitehorn, and the late Brian Redhead were regularly aired.[8] In April he was on Network Three again in a programme called *Education Today* and on the Midland Home Service talking about the vacant places at universities. He followed this up in September on *Tonight* with Ronald Kay talking about the wastefully high drop-out rates which many universities then had.[9] Both of these were topics featured in *Where?* magazine. This was all excellent publicity for ACE.

In November he spoke on television about religion in schools and reviewed two sociological texts in *The World of Books* while December found him comparing European and English education in *Education: Patterns for the Future*.[10] In 1964 he spoke on Oxbridge entrance, late starters, a second start in education, and in December he was interviewed by Brian Redhead for the BBC's Northern Home Service about teaching English.[11] This was in connection with his two short textbooks for junior schools: *Good English Prose* Books I and II. He appeared again with Brian Redhead on the latter's late-night radio talk series, *A Word in Edgeways* in March 1966.[12]

Meanwhile, in October 1963, as part of his launch of the NEC as a prototype for the Open University, Brian Jackson, together with Peter Laslett, had created *Dawn University* – the first experiment in using television for educational purposes – with a week-long series of lectures given by dis-tinguished academics.[13] This was followed in May and June 1964 by a series of programmes on Anglia TV for students of 'O'-level English and maths and in October of that year the BBC finally linked up with the NEC, but only very tentatively, by putting out a radio programme for 'O' level English on its Sutton Coldfield (old Midland Region) VHF transmitter. This brought the college publicity and 330 correspondence students but it led to a national radio series the following year which brought almost 2,000 more recruits together with a similar increase in enrolments for an 'A'-level English course.[14] These early excursions in broadcasting led to regular co-operation between NEC and radio and TV including, after the launch of the Open University, a series of 'Gateway' courses designed to prepare students with no previous academic background. By 1967 Brian Jackson was proposing linking universities internationally by television using satellites which were then just beginning to come on stream: *Intelstat III* was due to span the world by

1968 'with the possibility to reach African states that have no land-line systems by 1971'.[15]

Yet back in reality in 1967, and at a more basic level, Brian had set up a television series with the BBC's pioneer producer of programmes for Asian immigrants, David Gretton. The idea was that ACE, following the recommendations of Plowden, would start a nursery school for immigrant children in a deprived area as they had already done in relatively prosperous and articulate Cambridge. And because Asian women were not well integrated into their host communities the school would be televised on Gretton's *Apna Hi Ghar Samajhiye* (Make Yourself at Home) to show mothers what a school in England would be like for their children and learn, from a commentary in their own language, the importance of 'play, fantasy, child motivation'.[16] Such modern trends were thought to be unfamiliar from their own schooldays.[17] Sadly David Gretton died just as Brian had secured funding for the nursery from the Van Leer Foundation but the project went ahead and the nursery was named in Gretton's memory. It was the start of many schemes launched by Brian on behalf of immigrant and minority communities.

The most ambitious attempt that Brian ever made to harness the media in a good cause was his scheme to create a local radio station in Cambridge. It often appears that all Brian had to do to launch a project was to announce its formation with sufficient panache and the thing would then take off almost as if by magic. But behind the scenes there was a great deal more to it than that. Despite, or perhaps *because*, of the fact that Radio Cambridge never came to fruition, the archive contains a mass of detail on the background to it. It may be that the true reason for all the effort detailed in the archive was that Brian saw Radio Cambridge as an alternative to the Open University. At that stage it was not clear, as it is with hindsight, how successful the OU would be. Moreover Brian was already disappointed at the predominantly middle-class nature of its early intake. He may well, therefore, have believed that he could produce a truly classless cultural and educational service to rival the OU and thus assuage his disappointment at having his National Extension College, which he set up as a pilot for the OU, passed over. Whatever the reason this material is invaluable for the light it sheds on Brian's strategy and methods: putting his ideas to an ever-widening circle of friends, friends of friends, and acquaintances, for their comments, reaction and ideas.

When Christopher Chataway, the new Minister for Posts and Tele-communications announced, in 1970, that the Government was about to publish a White Paper with proposals for commercial radio Brian immediately began to make plans. He wrote to Chataway on 25 June 1970 to propose a non-commercial station linking such groups as extra-mural departments of the University, the Workers Educational Association, and NEC to 'promote the sorts of things they [NEC] and ACE were doing'.[18] He brought in John

Hipkin in July 1970, for a fee of £100 for six months, to examine the case for such a station.[19] Confirming this Brian wrote 'Just to set down our (I hope historic) conversation' and that the brief was 'to explore if a 'lobby' both national and in Cambridge could be organised.'[20] At the same time he sounded out various people including Conrad Halloran, the treasurer of NEC, who liked the idea but did not think it viable without advertisements, and Richard Blake, Executive Director of ACE, who said Cambridge had lots of good live music and proposed a local critics panel for cinema, theatre and musical events.[21] In August 1970 Brian received a cautious reply from the Postmaster's Office, apologising for the delay in answering and saying that they 'could not rule out a non-profit making station'.[22] In September John Hipkin reported progress so far, hoping Brian had a 'marvellous' time on holiday in Ireland, and Brian approached Nicholas Herbert, the editor of the *Cambridge Evening News*, and John Elven, the Town Clerk of Cambridge. During October Brian wrote to several people for support including Professor Sir Neville Mott, Chairman of the Trustees of the NEC, Frank Jaques of the WEA, and Tony Benn, who was very encouraging.[23] In November the campaign was carried to the aldermen of Cambridge, to David Piper, Director of the Fitzwilliam Museum and to Edmund Leach, the Provost of King's College who could not offer cash support but said the project sounded very exciting and invited Brian to 'come and talk'.[24] Brian reported to John Hipkin that Leach was a 'fussy old don' but that Polack (the Bursar) was 'very strong for it' and wanted to be on the committee.[25] John Elven was also very willing in his capacity as a public servant to help – Brian later described him as 'a good bloke . . . cautious but liberal' – and by February 1971 Brian was able to write to Chris Chataway to confirm that a committee had been formed.[26] This was the result of a meeting held on 19 January 1971.[27]

At the same time Brian announced in an article in *The Times* that as and when the government were ready 'we in Cambridge' would make a bid.[28] He went on

> We cannot have a BBC station [the council had refused to pay their share when one was proposed in 1966[29]]. We do not want a pop-and-advert station. We feel we ourselves can use our own airspace. For there is a third way – and we are requesting Mr Chataway to sanction, in Cambridge, an experiment in community broadcasting. If we are successful, this would clearly be an experiment of national interest which other cities might wish to consider and even imitate.

Although this was a very difficult time for Brian as the NEC was nearly crippled by the postal workers' strike the lobbying and local activity continued during the early months of 1971. Ken Polack formally joined the committee in a private capacity and David Lane, M.P. confirmed that John Elvin had notified him about the plans for Radio Cambridge.[30] An article in the *Cambridge Evening News* posed the question 'Commercial radio: Culture or canned music?' and the debate was taken up with enthusiasm within the University. Larry Cohen, a student at Emmanuel College sent Brian an article from the student paper *Stop Press*.[31] Tim Wheatley, a senior editor at the Cambridge University Press expressed cautious interest and said he would be prepared to ask the Syndics to help finance the project.[32] A second meeting of the committee on 8 April 1971 at ACE's offices on Trumpington Street considered, among other matters, the Government's White Paper and the legal status of Radio Cambridge, based on a Memorandum of Association drawn up by Peter Soar, solicitor to ACE.[33] In May ACE received a formal invitation from John Elven to join the council's Broadcasting Consultative Committee.[34] Brian Jackson was to be their representative and Richard Blake was to deputise in his absence.[35]

Brian's next move, having got the council to form an official committee, was to organise an informal meeting of as many public figures who might be interested in his proposed station as possible.[36] The local Chief Super-intendent of Police was keen to come, but the *Cambridge Evening News*, who possibly feared such a station would threaten their advertising revenue, were guarded, as was P. Threlfall, Managing Director of the local electronics company Pye whose main interest was that their equipment should be used whoever might run such a station.[37] Tim Wheatley wrote to say 'yes, send a sober outline of [your] plan' for the Syndics of the CUP while David Lane, MP, wrote to say 'Chataway says license will be for the Independent Broadcasting Authority to decide' so he could not 'push any more at the London end'.[38]

As a result of all this activity, and having commissioned a report at a fee of twenty-five guineas on feasibility from a firm called Independent Broadcasting Consultants, Brian submitted a request for financial support in some detail on behalf of the Cambridge Educational Development Trust. The request named the following personnel involved with CEDT in the application: Deryck Mumford, Principal, Cambridgeshire College of Arts and Technology, John Elven, Frank Jaques, WEA, Norman Higgins, Trustee of Cambridge Arts Theatre Trust, Vyvian Ramsbottom, Extramural Board, Ken Polack, Bursar of King's College, Peter Laslett, Fellow of Trinity College, David Piper, Director of the Fitzwilliam Museum, Brian himself as Director of ACE and ACE's solicitor, Peter Soar, of Wild Hewitson and Shaw. Both Ken Polack and Peter Soar were to play busy roles in subsequent events as was another recruit from that period, Ben Duncan, formerly a director of the London advertising agency Collett, Dickenson Pearce and Partners, who offered his services so that Brian would know what the opposition were likely to be thinking.[39]

During September 1971 Tim Wheatley reported that he liked the draft proposal which he intended to present to the Syndics on 24 September and the independent consultants reported that it was important to establish urgently who was to own the new station and where the financial backing was to come from. John Elven, thanking Brian for a courteous note about a meeting he had arranged 'beautifully' remarked dryly that he 'had the not-unique experience of feeling that we could have reached the same predictable conclusions by a shorter route.'[40] At the end of the month Brian wrote thanking Tim Wheatley for the £250 to cover expenses already incurred and remarking that it was splendid news that the Syndics might consider a direct holding (in the station).[41]

In the following couple of months Ben Duncan worked on his ideas for possible advertising revenues. Brian reported that David Groombridge, the Educational Secretary to the IBA reckoned that the invitations to tender from the ITA 'would not preclude' one from a trust such as CEDT, though this was hedged around with the 'usual "ifs" and "buts", etc.' but also with an encouraging 'keep in touch'.[42] By late January 1972 Brian was beginning to write round seeking finance for his new station and circulating a draft plan and feasibility study.[43] Among several congratulatory replies – and a few rather more lukewarm ones – was Tony Benn's 'I think yours is far and away the most highly developed alternative possibility to the regular commercial station, and I think your idea of a mixed revenue is a most sensible one.'[44]

However, a note of internal dissent was sounded in March 1972 when Richard Blake reported to Brian – who missed it through illness – on a meeting of the council's Broadcasting Consultative Committee on Tuesday 29 February 1972. John Hipkin had attended as the CEDT representative and despite a vague resolution welcoming a station with 'wide interests' it was, in Richard's view 'hardly successful' as the business side had tried to avoid having Brian's paper discussed. Worse, John Hipkin had gone 'too far in his rather aggressive manner and even attacked the chairman at one point'. John Elven had to leave before the end but up to then had 'guided' the (rather lost) chairman.[45] Elven himself reported much the same message, but in suitably official language, whilst the *Cambridge Evening News* finally declared its hand and, fearing for its advertising revenues, threw in its lot with a rival commercial group, Force Three Associates.[46] To make matters worse John Thompson, Advisor Radio, ITA, wrote to thank Brian for the plan but said 'as I am sure you realise . . . there is a long way to go . . . local radio [is] likely to be phased in over the next few years.'[47]

Nothing daunted, in April 1972 Brian arranged a sherry party and wrote to several people and organisations inviting their financial support including Lord Walston, a local landowner and former Labour Minister who was Chairman of the East Anglia Planning Board.[48] He was interested and gave Brian several other people to contact as did Sir Kenneth Berrill, Chairman of the University Grants Committee and a former ally from NEC fund-raising days. Indeed he went further and wrote to several masters of Cambridge colleges to ask if Brian might meet them.[49] Harry Walston, as he quickly became in correspondence with Brian, 'lunched with Durham' deputy Chairman and Managing Director of *Cambridge Evening News*, but could not get them to relent. However a rather stiff reply by Durham to a subsequent letter from Brian said they proposed to lead a consortium of interests when and if the government decided Cambridge was a suitable location and they were 'glad to have seen your proposals' and would 'consider if there is any basis for co-operation'[50]

Sir Kenneth Berrill also involved G. Williams, Chief Executive Officer of Cambridge Co-op, during May 1972, stressing that the new station should be 'town' as well as 'gown', while Peter Soar, with comments from Ken Polack, was busy re-drafting the constitution of the proposed station which was now intended, as Brian wrote to Reuben Heffer of the bookshop, to be a profitable enterprise returning 'modest, but not excessive, dividends.'[51] Sir Geoffrey de Freitas wrote in June to say he was interested in putting up £10,000 and proposed that five local citizens and five colleges should be encouraged to do likewise to fund the station.[52] Brian was visiting Australia and calling at Bangladesh on the way home during June and a note of gloom appeared in a letter to Julia McGawley, who was holding the fort in his absence, that it seemed Cambridge was not, after all, to have a radio station for 'some while to come'.[53] This was echoed by Ken Polack who also wrote to Brian on his return in July saying 'I take it the project will have to go into cold storage for some years'.[54] This followed the official metamorphosis of the Independent Television Authority into the Independent Broadcasting Authority in July 1972.[55]

But within a week Peter Soar was writing to say what good news it was that Sir Geoffrey de Freitas was interested, and that he, Peter, had re-worked the articles of association. It is clear from this letter that despite acknowledging that the Cambridge proposals looked 'extremely interesting', the IBA had decided not to approve a station for the city.[56] Still undaunted, Brian phoned the IBA who confirmed that there was 'no reason to stop anyone from outside the nominated areas making an approach.'[57] His letter to Ken Polack continued 'Indeed, they expect our approach to be somewhat unconventional . . . so let's press on with the lunch on 4 August – a new group of people ready to finance a community-oriented station could emerge. . . .' Poor Peter Soar was busy re-drafting the articles yet again and he noted in a letter to Brian that 'things seem to be moving fairly swiftly'.[58] They did indeed. The lunch appears to have been a success as Brian was writing to several people on 7 August that they had raised some £60,000 of the £100,000 needed based on a 'commercial consortium but with 40 per cent of its holding in trust.'[59] He later confirmed what had been agreed at the lunch and reported back to various people including John Hipkin, Ben Duncan, Peter Soar, and Chris Kelly, later described as a local freelance broadcaster, who seems to have been brought in at this stage.[60] John Elven replied to this report that a firm proposal could be put to the Consultative Committee of the Council which could then 'lobby the IBA' and, he shrewdly remarked, 'could put pressure on other known interests a bit by asking them if they have any alternative proposals. . . .'[61]

Brian was away 'riding and writing in the West' during September but things were moving inexorably back in Cambridge.[62] Ben Duncan was to do an article for New Society while Chris Kelly's brief was to produce demonstration tapes. Mark Elwes invited the group, via Ben Duncan, to join the Local Radio Association and Mr Williams chipped in with information – 'fascinating figures . . . much more optimistic than ours' – about Plymouth Radio which the Co-op there had apparently helped to finance.[63] In October John Thompson, head of radio at the IBA, wrote to say he was very busy with the first contracts for the larger towns but would be glad to see Brian later in the Autumn or early in the New Year and in the meantime Brian deputed Ben Duncan to go ahead with his idea of commissioning a viability survey for Radio Cambridge. He also wrote to Ken Berrill inviting him to be one of the trustees who were to hold the 40 per cent stake in the new venture, and approached Tim Wheatley at the CUP who suggested that 'some of the newer people' might like to finance the next stage of the campaign.[64]

By November 1972 Brian was writing to John Elven with costings and was confident that 'the majority of the £100,000 capital required has been raised and we expect all of it to have been raised and the Cambridge Commercial Broadcasting Company to have been set up before Christmas.'[65] The capital was raised only in the sense of being promised, of course, but that was all that could be done until the IBA could be persuaded to grant a licence and Brian prepared a handout to the effect that two years after the original announcement in *The Times* the Cambridge Broadcasting Scheme was 'now ready to move into operation as soon as the IBA nominates our area and invites applications'.[66] Yet things were not all running smoothly. David Groombridge, head of educational programme services at the IBA commented that Brian's proposals 'smacked of knows-bestism' and were paternalistic, while Ken Berrill wrote to say that as a civil servant he regretted that he was unable to become a trustee. Undaunted, Brian was writing to assure the Hon. J.J. Astor, one of the new sponsors, about finding a station manager: 'If we create the first community radio . . . every young man wishing to make his name will be after us.'[67]

John Rhodes of the University's Department of Applied Economics wrote to Ben Duncan to say that the £200 fee proposed for a viability study was 'far too low' but he was prepared to produce something in his own time at the undergraduate teaching rate – then £3.50 an hour – and Duncan accepted this with alacrity, offering to undertake the advertising side himself.[68] John Hipkin wrote in December too, proposing a New Year party and in passing, referring to a review of children's books by Brian which had recently appeared in the *Guardian,* asked rather prophetically 'I sometimes feel that you'll leave the turbulent river of community politics and follow a gentler course! Will you?'[69] As Christmas loomed Brian wrote to John Thompson at the IBA saying they 'should have a viable scheme by the second half of January' while Lord Walston was drumming up support from contacts at Barclays Bank.[70]

On the first of January 1973 Brian wrote to Peter Soar saying he would like to present Cambridge Commercial Broadcasting Company to a meeting on 15 January 1973 with a capital of £200 capable of being expanded to £100,000, with Lord Walston as Chairman, and Ben Duncan, Ken Polack, G. Williams, Chris Kelly, John Hipkin and Brian himself as directors. But in late January Brian wrote to Norman Higgins about the constitution of the Arts Theatre Trust saying that it looked as if Cambridge Radio might 'yet become an all-trust station'.[71] Higgins kind and prompt reply referred to that trust's thirty-five year history, offered advice gladly, and intimated that they might even be interested in taking shares in the new venture.[72] In the course of the next few days Brian wrote to Lord Walston to say Chris Kelly was 'prepared to be station manager', reported to the members of his group, and, thanking Norman Higgins, said he was just off north for a while.[73]

Despite Brian's absence he kept in touch. Chris Kelly produced his demo tape – 'the wit and wisdom of David Lane' – and looked forward to meeting Lord Walston.[74] Peter Soar re-drafted the articles yet again in response to points raised by Ken Polack and, looking forward to seeing the Arts Theatre's Trust Deed 'as promised', recommended taking counsel's advice on it.[75] Steve Harris of the Bradford *Telegraph and Argus* wrote to Peter Soar asking for a copy of the Cambridge articles. They were proposing to bid for a community station in Bradford and time was short as the town had already been selected by the IBA. Brian wrote to commiserate with Doreen Stephens who was to have been Rediffusion's station manager in their unsuccessful bid for London Radio, inviting her to come to lunch to brief them on how, or possibly how *not*, to frame an application to the IBA.[76] She replied that the IBA 'fell for the glamour of Dickie Attenborough and Bryan Forbes', and invited Brian up to London to 'go through the papers'.[77]

In March, Ben Duncan sent Dr Rhodes' viability study off to Lord Walston in time for the company's first board meeting on 12 March 1973, after which Ken Polack raised yet another point with Peter Soar. Three days later Brian was reporting to several interested parties that the meeting had 'heard confirmation of pledges of financial support' and that 'since then [they had] made considerable progress with legal business'.[78] He followed this next month with the news that Lord Walston had given a lunch for John Thompson of the IBA at which he and Ben Duncan were present and after a 'vigorous discussion all emerged with the feeling that a unique proposal like ours was very much welcomed. We agreed to put a paper to the IBA arguing the case for a relatively early decision about Cambridge.'[79]

After that the rest is silence except for a note nearly a year later in March 1974 from Ken Polack to Brian saying that in the light of a recent meeting with Radio Bradford (subsequently Pennine Radio), Radio Cambridge 'does not look at all viable'.[80] Brian valiantly replied that he thought Bradford's figures were wrong and that the new government, 'in which we all have so many excellent connections' was at least a promise for a breakthrough.[81] But of course Brian had been back in Yorkshire for nearly a year by then. He had moved to Elland on his appointment as Simon Research Fellow at Manchester University the previous Autumn.

Why did Brian Jackson leave Cambridge? Was it through disappointment and frustration at the failure of this scheme, into which he had put so much effort? And did he pursue it so relentlessly because, disgruntled at having been by-passed by Jenny Lee when she created the Open University that he first proposed, and for which he had done so much pioneering work, he was determined to create some sort of alternative cultural-educational institution? It seems that, unlike Ken Polack, Brian never accepted that his scheme was, in the words of his friend, the former academic and television presenter and one of Radio Bradford's founders, Austin Mitchell MP, 'just plain daft'.[82] Mitchell's wide professional experience of the media confirmed treasurer Halloran's original assessment that the station would not be viable without the revenue from advertisements.[83] This is almost certainly the reason the attempt was a failure. It would seem that Brian's altruism had led him to pursue the idea well beyond what might have been thought to be the bounds of reason.

Brian may have left Cambridge because he felt, as a result of his experiences with the Priority Playgroup in Birmingham and with ACE's Priority project in Liverpool, his future lay with helping the very young. Possibly he just wanted to get back to his roots and to refresh his reserves. Certainly he was not finished with campaigning. And, as the next decade would show, he was by no means finished with the media. Some of his greatest triumphs were yet to come.

Notes

1. Huddersfield College. Brian Anthony Jackson, Age 15 y. 11 m., Xmas Term, 1948.
2. Nor was this the only such occasion, Interview with Frank Pedley, 11 June 1996.
3. Contracts with the BBC and others, 1962-66, H18.
4. *idem.*
5. *idem.*
6. *idem.*
7. *idem.*

8. *idem.*
9. *idem.*
10. *idem.*
11. *idem.*
12. *idem.*
13. 'Dawn University', *Where?*, 17 Summer 1964.
14. 'The Invisible College NEC 1963-1979', International Extension College Broadsheet on Distance Learning: 15, p.64.
15. 'Linking Universities by Satellite', *Where?*, 34, November 1967.
16. 'An ACE nursery for immigrant children', *Where?*, 31 May 1967.
17. *idem.*
18. Letter to Christopher Chataway, 25 June 1970, F14.
19. Letter to David Baron, NEC, 27 July 1970, F14.
20. Letter to John Hipkin, 24 July 1970, H13.
21. Letter from Conrad Halloran, 27 July 1970, F14. Letter from Richard Blake, 28 July 1970, H13.
22. Letter to Brian Jackson, 11 August 1970, F14.
23. Letter to Tony Benn, 19 October 1970. Letters from Tony Benn to Brian Jackson, 22 October, and 10 November, 1970. F14.
24. Letters to aldermen and to David Piper, 12 November 1970. Letter from Edmund Leach to Brian Jackson, 18 November 1970. F14.
25. Letter to John Hipkin, 1 December 1970, F14.
26. Letter to Sir Nevill Mott, 26 May 1971. Letter to Chris Chataway, 2 February 1971, F14.
27. Minutes of second meeting, 8 April 1971, F14.
28. 'The Cambridge Experiment', *The Times*, 15 February 1971.
29. Report *Cambridge Evening News*, 28 April 1972. H14.
30. Letter from Ken Polack, 22 February 1971. Letter from David Lane, 25 February 1971, F14.
31. Press cutting *Cambridge Evening News* 23 April 1971. Letter from Larry Cohen, 4 February 1971, H14.
32. Letter from Tim Wheatley, 16 April 1971, F14.
33. Minutes of second meeting of committee, 8 April 1971, F14.
34. Letter from John Elven, Town Clerk, 17 May 1971, F14.
35. Letter to John Elven, 21 May 1971, F14.
36. Letters and replies re meeting 22 June 1971, F14.
37. Brian Jackson to John Hipkin, 6 July 1971, F14.
38. Letters from Tim Wheatley, 9 July 1971, and David Lane, 19 July 1971, F14.
39. Letter from Ben Duncan, 31 August 1971, F14.
40. Letters from Tim Wheatley, 3 September 1971, Independent Broadcasting Consultants, 17 September 1971, John Elven, 17 September 1971 in reply to Brian Jackson's letter 14 September 1971, F14.
41. Letter to Tim Wheatley, 29 September 1971, F14.
42. Letters to John Elven and John Hipkin, 8 December 1971, F14.
43. Letters from Brian Jackson, 21-24 January 1972, F14.
44. Letter from Tony Benn, 3 February 1972, F14.
45. Report from Richard Blake, 1 March 1972, F14.
46. Hand-written memo from Barrie Knight, 20 March 1972. Letter from John Elven, 20 March 1972, F14.
47. Letter from John Thompson, Ministry of Posts and Telecommunications, 20

March 1972, F14.

48. Report to colleagues by Brian Jackson 11 April 1972, H15.

49. Letters form Sir Kenneth Berrill, 27 April 1972, H15.

50. Letters to Brian Jackson, 26 April 1972, and 1 May 1972, H15.

51. Letter from Peter Soar, 5 May 1972, Letter from Sir Kenneth Berrill to G. Williams, 24 May 1972, Letter to Reuben Heffer, 31 May 1972, H15.

52. Letter from Sir Geoffrey de Freitas, 6 June 1972, H15.

53. Letter from Nicolas Melersh, Rediffusion, 21 June 1972, H15.

54. Letter from Ken Polack, 13 July 1972, H15.

55. Press notice, 12 July 1972, H14.

56. Letter from Peter Soar, 17 July 1972, H15.

57. Letter to Ken Polack, 20 July 1972, H15.

58. Letter from Peter Soar, 28 July 1972, H15.

59. Several letters from Brian Jackson, 7 August 1972, H15.

60. Report by Brian Jackson, 17 August 1972, H15.

61. Letter from John Elven, 24 August 1972, H15.

62. Letter from Brian Jackson, 5 September 1972, H15.

63. Letters to Ben Duncan and Chris Kelly, 7 September 1972, and from Mark Elwes, 14 September 1972, and to G. Williams, 19 September 1972, H15.

64. Letter from John Thompson, 10 October 1972. Letter to Ben Duncan, 12 October 1972. Letter to Ken Berrill, 18 October 1972. Letter from Tim Wheatley, 25 October 1972, H15.

65. Letter to John Elven, 10 November 1972, H13.

66. Handout, November 1972, H13.

67. Letter from David Groombridge, 6 November 1972. Letter from Ken Berrill, 29 November 1972. Letter to Hon. J.J. Astor, 30 November 1972, H15.

68. Letter from John Rhodes, 6 December 1972. Letter from Ben Duncan, 7 December 1972, H15.

69. Letter from John Hipkin, 9 December 1972, H15.

70. Letter to John Thompson, 15 December 1972. Letter from Lord Walston, 20 December 1972, H15.

71. Letter to Norman Higgins, 22 January 1972, H15.

72. Letter from Norman Higgins, 23 January 1973, H15.

73. Letters to Lord Walston, 29 January 1973, and to Norman Higgins, 30 January 1973, H15.

74. Letter from Chris Kelly, 5 February 1973, H15.

75. Letter from Peter Soar, 14 February 1973, H15.

76. Letter from Steve Harris, 16 February 1973. Letter to Doreen Stephens, 22 February 1973, H15.

77. Letter from Doreen Stephens, 8 March 1973, H15.

78. Letter from Ben Duncan, 8 March 1973; letter from Ken Polack to Peter Soar, 13 March 1973; letters from Brian Jackson, 16 March 1973, H15.

79. Letters from Brian Jackson, 5 April 1973, H15.

80. Letter from Ken Polack, 1 March 1974, H15.

81. Letter from Brian Jackson, 18 March 1974, H15.

82. Interview with Austin Mitchell, 9 November 1996.

83. *idem.*

Chapter 6
Into the 1970s

While Brian Jackson was attempting to create a community radio station in Cambridge he was involved in several other projects and schemes simultaneously. In addition to writing regularly in *Where?* and producing several pamphlets reporting on ACE's various practical projects he was busy setting up the Liverpool Priority project with Eric Midwinter. Above all, he seems to have been desperately trying to set up a major project of his own independent of ACE. By securing a grant from the Social Science Research Council in 1973 he finally succeeded.

In this chapter I want to look at events leading up to that break. Brian went to great lengths to defend ACE and *Where?* for allegedly supporting the notorious *Little Red Schoolbook*. He wrote a major article in the *New Statesman*, criticising the record of the Labour Governments of the 1960s on education. He was approaching forty and these actions show that he was increasingly seeing himself, with some justification, as a public figure. His series of pamphlets describing the past decade's activities at ACE have a valedictory air and his increasing pre-occupation with the pre-school years all suggest that he was ready for a change.

The struggle to save the National Extension College from collapse during its difficulties of 1970-71 and Brian's key role in its rescue is documented elsewhere. It is typical of his buoyant outlook that at the end of 1971 he cited 'winning direct government aid for an eight-year old college we had started with no money or staff in a builders hut', as one of the year's highlights.[1]

As the new decade dawned Brian reported in *Where?* the struggle to set up the priority area playgroup in Birmingham which, as Director of ACE, he had instigated.[2] Significantly, in view of the direction his future career was to take, he highlighted the problems of getting West Indian children to the playgroup, as many of their mothers were at work and needed, 'an arrangement whereby their children are cared for throughout the working day'.[3] In addition he wrote a regular chatty column of miscellaneous items in *Where?* from May to November 1970. In May he proposed that secondary and junior school teachers should swap places for a year so as to understand what it was like for children to move from one to the other. Quoting an imaginary form master of 2B; 'I don't know what they taught you in your primary school', he commented dryly, 'Indeed he doesn't. He's never been.'[4] Brian knew from his postbag that the magazine was read by teachers as well as parents and this was yet another example of his attempts to change the hidebound attitudes and practices prevalent among many in the profession. July's column included a detailed refutation of Sir Cyril Burt's 'evidence' used in a *Black Paper* to suggest that educational standards had fallen since the time of the First World War, and in September Brian was lamenting, whatever the genetic effects on a child's ability, the dreadful inequality of opportunity amongst five-year olds due to the absence of any intellectual stimulation in the home lives of many of them before that age. 'Every £1 that we invest in the education of a pre-school child yields as much as £10 spent on a primary school child or £50 spent at the secondary stage. Except that we don't spend the first £1 at all.'[5] He went on to maintain that the waste of potential, as any reception class teacher could confirm, was colossal, and that 'even the best system of child-centred primary schools, unstreamed classes, and an open comprehensive system cannot win it back.'[6] Our folly, he continued, in failing to build a national system of nursery schools and playgroups – the cost of which he put at less than a fifth of the cost of Concorde – stunts our whole educational system, helping to translate social inequality into educational inequality . . . and . . . reduces the possible yield of the whole education system by something like a quarter to a third'[7]. This is not a scientific paper: he makes no attempt to justify his figures. Nor is it a direct plea for social engineering through education – he only claims a better performance for the system – but it points firmly towards the area in which his major efforts were subsequently to be directed.

The year 1970 was the centenary of W. E. Forster's Education Act which, in the words of Brian Simon, 'established a universal system of elementary schools for the working class'.[8] As Brian Jackson wrote in a review of an address on the centenary by Sir Alec Clegg, it was a bitter irony that the 'first real act of the Government after the centenary was to allow backward authorities to retain the 11-plus.'[9] The new Minister was Margaret Thatcher. It was a defining moment. Nevertheless, ACE was not going to throw in any towels. Announcing in the last issue of 1970 that from January 1971 *Where?* would become a monthly rather than a two-monthly magazine Brian wrote 'It is now quite clear that we cannot expect our schools, colleges and universities to go on expanding at the same rate. At the same time' he continued,

> The march of liberal ideas is challenged. Schoolmasters have seriously suggested that parents should pay them for Open Evenings, and other work out of school. Head teachers in several places have organised themselves to defend corporal punishment. Old ways of selecting children – like 11-plus or streaming – have received a new charge of life. And many people argue that not only cannot we afford to expand our universities, but that parents should more and more pay the cost of education, from nursery school fees to higher education vouchers out of their own pockets.[10]

In the first issue of the new-style *Where?* Brian wrote a piece 'On the Air: The end of a phase' with his colleagues Michael Young and Peter Laslett. This celebrated the birth of the Open University, whose first televised lecture was to be broadcast at 10.30 am on Sunday, 10 January 1971, and recounted how the National Extension College had pioneered this idea with a lecture given by Professor Fred Hoyle at '15 minutes past seven on the morning of 21 October 1963.'

The summer of 1971 was becoming hectic. David Holbrook, a friend and former collaborator with Brian Jackson and A.H. (Chelly) Halsey in 1963 on an ill-fated Fabian pamphlet; *Three Blasts of the Trumpet*, took great exception to what he alleged to be *Where?'s* endorsement of the notorious *Little Red Schoolbook*. This publication included, in addition to much sensible and practical information for children on other matters, some fairly straight-talking information about drugs and sex. The trouble started when *Where?* published its 'Charter for Children' in issue number 56, April 1971. This claimed for children, amongst other things, the right 'at appropriate age, to such knowledge as is necessary to understand the society in which they live. This shall include knowledge of sex, contraception, religion, drugs including alcohol and tobacco, and other problems which openly confront every growing child'.[11] It was this, as Brian later reported to Michael Young, which 'produced David Holbrook's very unpleasant leading article in the *Sunday Times* to which we replied through the correspondence columns.'[12] Holbrook's campaign appears to have been motivated by genuine ethical reservations although his friendship with Brian, based on their common ideas about education in many areas, was certainly tempered by a personal distaste for Brian's manners. Holbrook found him 'bumptious' and remembers taking some exception to Brian's commandeering the wine when a dinner guest at his house.[13]

Holbrook was not the only one to object. The archdeacon of Canterbury was taken to task by Brian Jackson in a letter to *The Times*, 4 May 1971 for his 'somewhat hot-blooded attack' on ACE's draft children's rights charter.[14] By 16 June 1971 Holbrook was writing to Brian; 'I know you will consider my reaction to the Children's Charter "hysterical". I haven't seen the last letter from ACE in the *Sunday Times* and don't want to . . .' he then continued for a full three pages criticising Leila Berg for praising the *Little Red Schoolbook* in *Where?* on the grounds that it promoted 'perversions' such as oral sex. In fact, Mrs. Berg was writing as a guest diarist in *Where?* and her views – she called it 'a lovely little reference book' – were clearly her own. Furthermore the gist of her article was that the police had confiscated all copies of the *LRSB* on 31 March from its publisher, Richard Handyside. Since Handyside was not charged until 13 April with 'possession of obscene material for gain' with the hearing set for 28 May 1971, it meant that if the second hearing was fixed for a further six weeks ahead, sales of the book would have been prevented for three and a half months without question of guilt having even been gone into. 'Is it any wonder young people become cynical, angry, aggressive?' she asked.[15] By July, with the trial of the *LRSB* progressing, Holbrook was becoming very agitated: 'I am so appalled and sickened by the spectacle of intellectuals going into the witness stand to proclaim that forms of education in dehumanisation are "harmless" that I cannot think in what way to protest.'[16] Both Brian and Beryl McAlhone, as editor of *Where?*, wrote placatory letters to Holbrook. 'We have had one or two other letters questioning Leila Berg's endorsement of *LRSB* in *Where?*' and so, Beryl continued, having stressed Mrs. Berg's independence as guest diarist, 'We have asked twelve ACE members from the *Where?* reading panel to give their opinion in the September edition of the magazine.[17] But by return Holbrook wrote 'Dear Beryl McAlhone, I'm afraid this reply of yours is not good enough. . . .' and for a further three pages he complained bitterly that he 'a poet, a novelist, and also a literary critic' was being censored by *Where?* and, protesting that he was a 'progressive' – indeed he was at the time employed at Dartington, largely, as it transpired, on Brian Jackson's recommendation – claimed that it was 'fanatical' of them to refuse to publish a letter 'on this important issue . . . from someone of my reputation'.[18] In the meantime Holbrook was writing to Sir Neville Mott and various Vice Chairmen of ACE to stir up opposition to the editorial line. He had some success. The *Times Educational Supplement* carried an article in August 1971 confirming that the Archbishop Beck of Liverpool had resigned from ACE over the issue of 'pornography'.[19] Both Brian Jackson and Eric Midwinter tried unsuccessfully to dissuade him.[20] Lord James of Rusholme also resigned but later retracted 'when he tumbled what was going on'.[21]

Holbrook stepped up his campaign in September with a long letter to all ACE Vice-Chairmen and a covering letter which not only described his various publications in some detail but also made much of his forthcoming publication *English in Australia* which railed against too much license in progressive teaching of English Literature there 'under the influence of "underground" ideas from America'.[22] Richard Blake, however, in Brian's absence on holiday, had pre-empted this by himself writing to all ACE's Vice Chairmen in late August prompted partly by a letter from Sir Nevill Mott to Beryl McAlhone saying Holbrook had misquoted him and was being made to acknowledge the fact.[23] Brian, who appears to have been getting rattled by Holbrook's campaign, followed this with a further circular letter enclosing a copy of Holbrook's article which, he said, was 'reasonably refused' on the grounds that it had not been invited, was on a subject 'we had not opened' and, moreover, was strongly suspected of seeking free publicity for his forthcoming book.[24]

The September issue of *Where?* duly carried the verdicts of the twelve ACE members but prior to its publication ACE issued the piece as a press release with a statement of its position (Appendix 1). The statement explained that their purpose was to give dispassionate and accurate advice to pupils, parents and teachers and that they felt there were subjects critical to young people where frank and informed discussion was lacking at school and at home. Pornography, they said, was *not* one of the major problems facing children. Nevertheless they had studied the *Little Red Schoolbook* and also sent it to a random group of ACE parents. The consensus, according to the article, was that the book contained much useful information on 'streaming, marks, homework, school buildings and participation' and that it offered a stimulating argument from which children would gain much. It said the section on sex education was weakened by its decision not to discuss human feelings but the only consistent charge that could be levelled against the book was its tendency to polarise the views of young and old. The only result of suppressing the book would, it maintained, be to confirm this feeling. Moreover copies would circulate even more widely among children and would be given a glamour they previously lacked.

ACE's conclusion was that the heated discussion about pornography was doing little service to education. The censoring of the *Little Red Schoolbook* was an unnecessary act, almost certain to have the opposite effect to that intended. It was out of line with the views of parents they had consulted who had actually read the book in full.'

The affair was a difficult one for ACE as *Where?* needed to be seen as the responsible adult publication of a serious educational organisation. Yet at the same time it was aware that the majority of its readership was, like its young editorial staff, likely to be more sympathetic to the *Little Red Schoolbook* than Holbrook was. Moreover although Leila Berg was officially only a 'guest diarist' her radical views (she wrote the book *Death of a Comprehensive* about the closure of Risinghill) were widely known. Brian was obviously concerned for the reputation of *Where?* and the issue of ACE's statement, backed up by the comments of 'a random group' of parents who were readers shows him to have been keenly aware of the possible political implications of Holbrook's campaign. He sent a 'file of papers' through to Peter Soar with a view to taking legal action against David Holbrook and the gist of the cool, and carefully reasoned reply was that since Holbrook was beginning to sound paranoid a court would be unlikely to be sympathetic and the best course was a dignified silence.[25] Happily, in a hand-written reply, Brian took the 'good advice'.[26]

Edward de Bono, however, whom Holbrook also criticised for giving evidence in support of the *LRSB* and *Oz,* was not so accommodating, and his lawyers forced a retraction from Holbrook to be circulated to all ACE's Vice Chairmen and in letters to *The Times* and *Guardian* newspapers, as Brian gleefully reported to Michael Young later.[27]

Though Brian was clearly upset by Holbrook's potentially damaging campaign the affair did have its lighter side. In April 1971 Stephen Corrin wrote to the *Times Educational Supplement* questioning the propriety of Holbrook's publishing a poem of his own which allegedly described his wife undressing in a possibly pornographic way whilst criticising others for purveying their own particular brand of sexuality.[28] And in June, Leonard Buckley writing an article headed 'Media' in the *Times Educational Supplement* referred to a letter in the *New Statesman* from a teacher who, being worried about pornography in a book he had bought for the school library was relieved to hear that David Holbrook, 'the well-known educationalist', was campaigning against just that. The sting was the book's author: David Holbrook.[29]

It is clear that by now Brian was becoming politicised and aware of himself as a public figure of some responsibility. In June 1971 he wrote a two-page article for the *New Statesman* rather grandly entitled 'Where Labour Went Wrong' reviewing the achievements and failures of the Wilson Governments of 1964-70 in education.[30] Comparing the nine months it took Labour to decide that the 11-plus was to be 'talked' rather than legislated 'out of existence' with the few days Margaret Thatcher needed to announce a mixed education system, he suggested that, despite increasing the education budget so that by 1970 it had overtaken defence spending for the first time in our history, Labour had 'misplayed the only big chance in education we have yet had'[31] In the context of the article the *we* clearly identified him as a Labour supporter and it is from this position that he analysed the Government's failures. Firstly, on pre-school education he said that the problem was referred to Plowden which 'largely played time out' and the great sadness was not only that little was done, but that no blueprint even existed to integrate playgroups, nursery schools and part-time schooling within a proper policy, including health and welfare, and based on children's centres. He denounced Labour's record on abolishing the 11-plus. He maintained that the Government had made a mockery of its espousal of comprehensive education by not providing cash to build the new larger schools. In any case, although they vilified the exam, many ministers who had themselves risen through the grammar schools on the old 'ladder of opportunity' as Sidney Webb described it, were reluctant to see them go: 'Over my dead body' was the Prime Minister's own response. Nor had Labour tackled what Anthony Crosland had described as 'much the most flagrant inequality of opportunity in our education system': the public schools. Once again it had referred the question to a Commission with the result that the public schools became 'the best charted and most minutely known schools in the country', but nothing was done about their integration into the state system. Indeed the Government even nudged the direct-grant schools a step nearer to total independence by including them in the referral.

Noting that it became harder under Labour to get into university as pressure for places built up, Brian criticised the Government's creation of a 'binary' system – two different systems of higher education of supposedly equal status. Anthony Crosland announced this policy in a speech at Woolwich Polytechnic and, in theory, Brian approved of the idea of producing graduate teachers and other technical personnel away from the rather stuffy and hidebound traditional universities which he believed would 'never develop applied studies on a sufficient scale, and in tune with the nation's needs'.[32] Yet although the polytechnics promised 'a new pattern of higher education based much more on the situation and needs of ordinary students' and despite the fact that, as Brian grudgingly admitted, 'Labour did focus attention on this major sector of education', the facilities in the polytechnics remained far poorer than in the universities. He quoted figures produced by the National Union of Students which showed that staff-student ratios were far lower (fewer staff in relation to numbers of students) in these institutions, as was expenditure on books, and concluded that despite his high hopes of a truly working-class system of higher education, the polytechnics were 'simply presented to the Conservatives [as] a low-cost overspill device'.[33]

Lastly, Brian was indignant that Labour had been cheeseparing. The Conservatives, under Edward Boyle, had proposed raising the school-leaving age but Labour had postponed the date. They had cut back on the school-building programme only to find that, being closely linked to comprehensivisation, it could not be delayed for ever and when resumed it faced increased costs. Ending free milk in secondary schools paved the way for Margaret Thatcher to scrap it altogether, which she did in 1971, and to challenge the principle of subsidised school meals for which Labour had fought so long and so hard. Unsurprisingly, his only praise for Labour's period in office was the establishment of the Open University, which he criticised for having a preponderance of middle-class students with GCE qualifications.

In a review of the events of 1971 Brian Jackson noted that 'Nothing was heard of yesterday's reports – Crowther, Robbins, Newsome, Plowden.' and that the efforts of ACE to promote improvements in home and school relations was also considered a thing of the past with progress being 'painfully slow.'[34] Another area where Brian regretted the fickleness of fashion was the Nuffield Science Project in junior schools which, he wrote, 'had left almost no trace at all'.[35] 'Things of Science', a branch of ACE, in conjunction with the *Sunday Times Magazine* ran a very successful environmental research project for children into pollution in rivers and streams. Some 10,000 children bought the simple testing kits and their findings were published in the newspaper in November 1971 as 'The Clean-River Report'. This project, as well as providing an interesting and educational experience for the children, also produced a useful and valid piece of scientific research.

Brian was also busy writing during 1971. He produced the booklet *1960-70: A Progress Report* which reviewed the first ten years of ACE's work.

One month later ACE brought out *100,000 Questions*, another booklet in which Richard Blake reviewed the work of ACE's advisory service and pinpointed the areas that had been shown to be of greatest need for information and outlined specific proposals for supplying this. A third report published by ACE in 1971 and co-written by Brian and Joan Jones, the Director of the Birmingham Playgroups Project, was *One Thousand Children*, which described the progress to date of the project, which by then had 14 day-care centres, nursery schools and playgroups serving over 400 children of many different ethnic backgrounds, and was increasingly being absorbed and funded by the local authority.

Describing ACE's work in 'Downtown Areas' Brian pointed out that 'Alongside the publications and advisory work stemming from Cambridge and serving largely a professional middle class audience of parents and teachers, ACE's involvement in direct work in poor urban areas is quite considerable.' He detailed the three main aspects of this work: The Association of Multi-Racial Playgroups, AMP; the Priority Area Playgroups Project in Birmingham; and the Priority project in Liverpool.[36] The role of the AMP, 'largely started by ACE and sustained by ACE' was to 'draw attention to the needs of under-fives in priority areas.'[37] It did this by holding one-day conferences in various parts of the country which brought local officials and voluntary workers together, and by publishing papers nationally.

The broadening of its scope from the original Birmingham project was signalled by AMP changing its name to Priority Area Children, PAC. After a special survey of pre-school provision in Liverpool: *Liverpool and its Under Fives,* by Kevin Shea, a deputation had been to see the minister responsible for such children. As a result of what Brian described as the 'rather sad and negative results' of this meeting he published the paper he had prepared for the meeting, *What did Lord Butler say in 1944?*, which criticised the lack of any government pre-school policy since the end of World War II and made proposals for such a policy.[38] The report quoted the work of Samuel Kirk on the effects of environmental stimulation – he claimed a good environment could raise a child's IQ from 80 to as much as 120 – and quoted Lord Butler's promise of nursery schools for all. Yet, as Brian reported, numbers of places in nurseries had dropped, not risen, from 72,000 at the end of the War to only 20,000 then, despite the call in the Plowden report of 1966 for increased provision of nursery education. The booklet, which contained comments on Brian's proposals from Edward Britton, General Secretary of the National Union of Teachers, Tessa Blackstone and Willem van der Eyken, author of *The Pre-School Years,* was reviewed widely by the Press. Philippa Ingram, writing in the *Times Educational Supplement,* noted Brian's fears that straight provision of nursery places on demand would be likely to benefit middle-class children rather than those in educational priority areas whose need was greater.[39] Pleading for provision to start in the EPAs under the Urban

Aid programme and expand outwards from there, Brian also commented on the growing numbers of children whose mothers went out to work and who were in day care. He proposed that day care should have 'an active educational content' and suggested closer links with nursery schools and playgroups especially for unregistered childminders who should be brought out into the open and supported rather than punished.[40]

This last was, doubtless, a reference to the findings of a survey that Sonia Jackson had just completed for the Cambridge Educational Development Trust, CEDT. As noted elsewhere (*ACE: The First Ten Years*) Brian had suspected that many West Indian children were not appearing at the Birmingham playgroups because they were spending long hours with childminders, many of whom were not legally registered. He began to sound out the possibilities of conducting research into 'such a delicate subject' in the summer of 1970.[41] Brian started to look for funding for the project and the Eva Reckitt Trust put up £250 for Sonia and Kevin Shea to do a pilot investigation. They prepared a 32 page report of their findings in November 1970. Sonia subsequently carried out a more detailed survey which was published the following November and aroused a considerable amount of attention in the Press.[42] National newspapers including *The Times, Guardian, Telegraph, Mirror, Mail, Morning Star*, all had pieces based on her report on 4 November 1971 as did the leading provincials: *Yorkshire Post, Wolverhampton Express and Star, Western Daily Press* of Bristol, Ipswich's *East Anglian Daily Times, Nottingham Guardian-Journal* and *The Journal* of Newcastle-on-Tyne. *New Society*, which came out that day, also featured Sonia's findings and during the next few days the *Times Educational Supplement*, *Teacher's World, Teacher*, and several provincial papers carried articles which referred to Sonia's report.[43] Its main conclusion was that large numbers of West Indian children were with illegal childminders but that, rather than prosecuting them, the childminders should be encouraged to come out into the open and given support with toy libraries, day nurseries, and decent – possibly government subsidised – rates of pay.

This met with a good deal of hostility as Brian reported in a letter to Lesley Garner of the *Sunday Times Magazine* who wrote the text which accompanied a pictures feature by Snowdon on black children in Birmingham in March 1972 entitled 'Black is Bored': 'Julia and I scouted the Birmingham patch but ran slap into hostility. Nobody wants publicity.'[44] Not the least of the hostility to Brian's early investigations came from his colleague, Joan Jones, who wrote enclosing a letter from Danny Lawrence, a lecturer in sociology at Nottingham University, 're money for the childminding project . . . and now I will leave it alone.'[45] It seems Jones felt the possibility of racial capital being made out of Sonia's report made her position in a multi-racial area much more difficult and she appears to have made her criticisms known to the Van Leer Foundation who sponsored the Birmingham Playgroup Scheme she controlled and which Brian was trying to persuade to fund more action research into illegal childminding. Brian's response was to notify other members of the ACE team of her actions saying that she was 'intoxicated by [Van Leer's] jet age treatment' and had 'poured out all her problems, views of ACE and PAP to senior Van Leer staff in a very disloyal way', and to offer to let Van Leer deal directly with her in future.[46] This was probably a bluff but Brian added that it looked as though they had lost the chance of the £30,000 grant he had been seeking. Subsequent letters from Brian to various other charitable trusts confirm this.[47] As noted earlier, however, there appears to have been a personal side to this row. Joan Jones had until then been on very good terms with Brian and been a frequent visitor to the ACE office in Cambridge.[48] Whatever the cause, their relations had obviously cooled.

Then in the summer of 1972 there was a breakthrough in the form of a letter from Stella Shaw, of the Social Science Research Council, regretting that an application for funding submitted on 6 April 1972 had been refused. The letter urged, however, that it be re-submitted with the inclusion of lots of technical sociological detail and proposed the addition of an educational psychologist to the team to add *gravitas* to the project.[49] The original application, which included Sonia's report and a copy of *1000 Children*, set out Brian's ideas very clearly and firmly. 'All previous research [into childminding] has had a medical orientation . . . [the] purpose of this is to see if a problem which has proved wholly resistant to research and legislation based exclusively on concerns of safety and health, might not yield to enquiry shaped in educational terms. . . . Instead of ignoring the growth of illegal childminding . . . we could . . . draw it, more hopefully, into the sphere of pre-school education. . . .'[50] This was the beginning of a realistic approach to a problem which offered the possibility of a cheap and cost-effective solution to the educational deprivation of thousands of under-fives. Sadly, a generation later, the problem still exists.

The application was duly re-submitted in September 1972 and signed, curiously enough as it was to be the foundation of the Cambridge, later National, Research and Development Trust, by Richard Blake as executive director of ACE but with a rather terse covering letter from Brian which includes the following: 'I think we did in fact accept all the committee's suggestions. Not sure, but think so.' In another very short paragraph he wrote, 'There's always a difference I think between earthy schemes and library ones.'[51] Shaw's assistant Gill Townend wrote back asking Brian to confirm that, as in his previous application, Eric Midwinter and Richard Blake would be running ACE while Brian worked on the new project. Finally, on 12 January 1973, a grant of £10,760 was approved subject to Brian's compliance with SSRC standard terms, to carry out a pilot study into the 'Educational Implications of Illegal Childminding, with Particular reference to West Indian Children'.[52]

This was, finally, the start of Brian's independent project but it was not the end of the needle match between him and Shaw. Although the SSRC's Information Officer, Francis Terry, had written to Brian in January 1973 saying they would 'leave the publicity to you' Shaw wrote a letter in April about the amount of publicity Brian was getting. She acknowledged that it was his own business, especially about research done before the SSRC grant was confirmed, but worried about the (adverse?) effect 'when you do begin in October this year.'[53] Brian's reply was a classic.

Thanks for your note.

Yes the announcement was very well received. News bulletins on radio and TV all carried it, and the BBC referred to it as 'a most imaginative grant . . .' and of course acres of news coverage everywhere . . . cuttings to your Information Officer Francis Terry and hope that in some small way this helps the Council's image and position. . . . A second advantage has been the large correspondence we've received . . . considerable range of people who are interested in the subject at one level or another . . . talking with [whom] should considerably enrich anything we have to say.

So by and large we are pleased that so modest a grant has received a warm and useful welcome. . . .[54]

Brian frequently found the civil-service mentality tiresome and, as this letter shows, he was quite prepared to let them know it. This grant funded Dawnwatch and all that followed from it. Brian took with him initially Barrie Knight, Julia McGawley, Anne Garvey and Sonia Jackson, and the research subsequently gave birth to both the book: *Childminder* and to the National Children's Centre in Huddersfield, the substance of another chapter.

It was the end of an era. Brian Jackson was leaving Cambridge, the scene of so many triumphs and quite a few disappointments, after nearly twenty years and returning to his Yorkshire roots. In his last few years as director of ACE he had demonstrated, by his vigorous defence of its reputation over Holbrook's attack, and by his broad *New Statesman* criticism of Labour's lack of achievements in the field of education, that he felt himself to be a national figure. The series of pamphlets he produced charting ACE's progress during the previous decade and his writings on the lack of provision for the under-fives indicate that he felt ready for a new challenge.

Notes

1. Brian Jackson, *Cambridge United, A 1971 progress report on ACE and NEC*, December 1971, p.3.
2. Priority Playgroups, *Where*, No. 47, January 1970, pp.18-21.
3. *ibid.*, p.21.
4. *Where?*, No.49, May 1970.
5. *Where?*, No. 51, September 1970.

6. *idem.*
7. *idem.*
8. Brian Simon, *Education and the Labour Movement 1870-1920*, p.11.
9. *Where?*, No. 52. November 1970.
10. *idem.*
11. Letter from Brian Jackson to Michael Young, 17 September 1971. F4.
12. *idem.*
13. Interview with David Holbrook, 15 October 1996.
14. *The Times,* 4 May 1971, Letter from Brian Jackson.
15. *Where?*, April 1971.
16. Letter to Brian Jackson, 13 July 1971, G14.
17. Letter from Beryl McAlhone, 16 July 1971, G14.
18. Letter to Beryl McAlhone, 18 July 1971, G14. Letter from Michael Young to Brian Jackson 9 September 1971, F4.
19. *Times Educational Supplement,* 27 August 1971.
20. Letter from Eric Midwinter to Archbishop Beck, 29 September 1971. Reply from the Archbishop, 1 October 1971 'I am already in correspondence with Brian Jackson. . .', G14.
21. Letter Brian Jackson to Michael Young, 17 September 1971, F4.
22. Circular letter from David Holbrook, 5 September 1971, F4. (the English magazine *Oz* was edited by an Australian, Richard Neville, at this time and also came in for a considerable amount of Holbrook's wrath – KH).
23. Circular letter from Richard Blake, 24/25 August 1971. Letter from Sir Nevill Mott, 19 August 1971, F4.
24. Circular letter from Brian Jackson, 3 September 1971, F4.
25. Letter from Peter Soar, 15 September 1971, G14.
26. Letter to Peter Soar, 18 September 1971, G14.
27. Letter to Michael Young, 4 November 1971, G14.
28. *Times Educational Supplement,* 23 April 1971.
29. *Times Educational Supplement,* 11 June 1971.
30. 'Where Labour Went Wrong', *New Statesman,* 4 June 1971.
31. *idem.*
32. *idem.*
33. *idem.*
34. Brian Jackson, *Cambridge United,* (ACE, December 1971).
35. *idem.*
36. Brian Jackson, *Cambridge United,* p.9.
37. *idem.*
38. *idem.*
39. Philippa Ingram, *Times Educational Supplement,* 14 January 1972.
40. Brian Jackson, *What Did Lord Butler Say in 1944?*, PAC, 1971, pp.5-7.
41. Letters, Brian Jackson to Winston Shaw, Gloucester Council for Community Relations, Carmen Brown, Kings Heath Birmingham, Douglas Tilbe, Race Relations Committee of the Society of Friends, 17 June 1970. E1/2.
42. Sonia Jackson, *The Illegal Childminders*, PAC, 4 November 1971. E8.
43. Newspaper cuttings, E1/2.
44. *Sunday Times Magazine,* 19 March 1972. Letter to Miss Lesley Garner, 17 November 1971. SJ1.
45. Memo from Joan Jones, n.d. enclosing letter from Danny Lawrence, 1 October 1970, E1/2.

46. Letter from Brian Jackson to ACE team, n.d. SJ1, Hazel Wigmore confirmed that no Van Leer money was subsequently forthcoming to the NCC, Interview, 28 July 1995.
47. Letters to Calouste Gulbenkian and reply from Richard Mills, 2 February 1972, and reply from Joseph Rowntree who felt it was not their subject and suggested Van Leer! SJ1.
48. Interview with Julia McGawley, 16 October 1996.
49. Letter from Stella Shaw, 30 June 1972, E1/2.
50. Copy of application to SSRC, E1/2.
51. Application submitted to SSRC, 29 September 1972, E1/2.
52. Letter from Gill Townend, 4 October 1972, E1/2. Press Release from Brian Jackson of CEDT, SJ3.
53. Letter from Miss Shaw 18 April 1973, E1/2.
54. Reply from Brian Jackson, 4 May 1973, E1/2.

Chapter 7
An Immense Influence[1]

Between setting up and running such organisations as the Advisory Centre for Education, the National Extension College, and later the National Children's Centre, and campaigning for other causes such as a community radio station for Cambridge, Brian Jackson was a prolific writer. It was just as well for towards the end of his life writing provided him with a major part of his modest income.[2] The wide range of his work reflects this need to earn money but more importantly illustrates the major preoccupations of his life. These fall into three broad themes. Brian wrote several serious books about education and children's welfare, as well as one which seems incongruous about two American anarchists. He produced thought-provoking and campaigning articles for the *New Statesman* and *New Society* and not least for the *Sunday Times Magazine*, in those early days a pioneering venture, which all the major papers subsequently copied. These latter pieces, especially, gained wide publicity for ACE. Thirdly, he combined a desire to reach a wider audience with a lucrative sideline by reviewing books and writing for popular magazines like *Living* and *Mother*. Throughout all Brian's work there runs an underlying current: the dichotomy between educated middle-class values and working-class culture, between self-help and co-operation, between Brian's boundless ambition and his roots. In this chapter I want to look at how these aspects of Brian's personality manifested themselves in his written work and what influence this had. Brian Jackson was, among other things, a very capable journalist who wrote at least two significant books.

The written word was probably the most important tool Brian used in his campaigning and he was good at it, writing, as his *Times* obituarist put it, 'Elegantly, with a deceptive simplicity, a memorable turn of phrase and pungent anecdote.'[3] And *The Times Educational Supplement* said, quoting Brian himself, that he 'Certainly had a way with words. His writing, in both posh and pop journals and magazines, was a powerful mixture of "personal experience, insight, academic reading and corn", as one of his friends put it.'[4]

It is through his writing that we can begin to understand the complex political animal that Brian Jackson was. He maintained he was always a committed and consistent socialist. Not for him the apostasy of joining the Social Democratic Party in the dark days of early Thatcherism. As Eric Midwinter reported, for Brian voting Labour was like supporting (Huddersfield) Town, you stuck with them through thick and thin.[5] But he was never remotely in sympathy with the bureaucratic centralism of Marx and Lenin. He championed freedom of choice for the individual and neighbourhood self-help schemes for small groups of the underprivileged. So much that Brian campaigned for and wrote about is still relevant today. It is this aspect of his politics that is most interesting. When Tony Blair was accused of stealing Baroness Thatcher's (political) clothes he rightly replied that he was doing no such thing, citing Ruskin, as Brian did, among others as his true political antecedents. Yet when, as Secretary of State for Education and Science in 1971, Margaret Thatcher rescued the National Extension College from the devastating effects of the postal workers' strike, she may well have been moved to support, in Brian Jackson, a fellow follower of Samuel Smiles and promoter of self-help. In 1967 he had written, in relation to the first four years' work at the NEC, 'Despite our vast and complex educational system, there is still room for enterprise . . .' and in an article on a similar theme he wrote that the experiment showed there was, 'still room for enterprise and self-help.'[6] Yet Brian Jackson's roots were in co-operation rather than competition. He maintained copying should not be punished; that was only a symptom of an over-competitive school. It should be encouraged as it leads to co-operation.[7] If that seems unorthodox in educational terms it is certainly in line with much management thinking. Despite a lifelong struggle to promote equality of opportunity, in which he achieved much, he never lost sight of the pursuit of excellence for all, which was the ultimate goal of the 'New Jerusalem' he longed for. As John Izbicki wrote in a personal memoir of the man he had known for 14 years, 'An ardent advocate of the comprehensive movement, he recently admitted that the system had been widely mishandled and that comprehensive school teachers had spent so much time trying to cater for the educationally backward child that they could not recognise the supremely gifted pupils in their classrooms.'[8]

That is where Brian Jackson's career as a writer and campaigner began: as a teacher in Whittlesford's William Westley Church of England Primary school near Cambridge and at the Brunswick School in the city itself between 1956 and 1960, he became fascinated with the creative writing abilities of quite young children if they were not inhibited by the constraints of grammar and the teaching of English in subservience to an easily-examinable curriculum.[9] From this experience he began to question conventional ideas about examinations for young children in general and early streaming as then practised from the age of seven in many primary schools. One result was the publication of what the contract in April 1961 called 'A primary English composition book' – *English in Education* – in conjunction with Denys Thompson, editor of the journal – *Use of English* – from which Brian's selection of extracts was taken. In 1963 he published two small textbooks – *Good English Prose Books I and II* – and on 16 September 1965 *English*

Versus Examinations, which sold 1,400 copies up to the end of that year. All these continued to bring in useful royalties during the 1960s. Perhaps it is time to re-issue *English Versus Examinations* as the argument, like so many of the subjects of Brian's campaigns, is still topical.

But Brian was becoming increasingly preoccupied with the sociology of education itself and, in 1960, he became a Senior Research Officer with the Institute of Community Studies and began to work with Dennis Marsden on the study of 88 working-class contemporaries of theirs – 90 strictly speaking as they were part of the sample themselves – which led to the publication on 2 February 1962 of *Education and the Working Class.* Some attempt to assess the influence of this book has been made elsewhere in terms of its huge paperback print run and wide and appreciative reception by students of education and the public in general. Dennis Marsden told me that strangers still slightly embarrass him by asking if he is *the* Dennis Marsden.[10] Another indication of its importance is that I found no less than 56 books which quoted from it in a random search of Huddersfield University's Education Campus Library.[11] Although an early reference was critical of its methodology most subsequent writers have acknowledged its importance. Geoffrey Bantock described its aim as 'impressionistic' and wrote that even that aim was 'marred by its emotionally charged repudiation of middle-class values and its largely uncritical acceptance of working-class virtues.' He maintained that 'beneath a surface appearance of fairmindedness' it revealed the authors' conviction that the grammar school must be wrong.[12] On the other hand F.T. Willey noted that they had 'convincingly demonstrated . . . [that] the abolition of fees had not changed the essential character of the grammar schools', and Morrison and McIntyre refer to their 'vivid' demonstration of even caring parents' ignorance of educational opportunities.[13] The book is described elsewhere as an 'impressionistic but telling account' of home-school conflicts suffered by working-class children at grammar schools and as a 'classic' account by 'influential writers' of the differences in educational achievement between social classes.[14] The book's identification of the importance of parental concern, albeit mostly evidenced by the middle-class control group they surveyed, was taken up by an American writer who commented that this was largely ignored in American sociology of education.[15] Like any major seminal work it had its critics too. F. Musgrove, discussing the 'fascinating problem', raised by Floud, of assimilating working-class children into the 'distinctive middle-class tradition' of the grammar school wrote that it was 'a theme which became shrill in sociological literature' and 'reached a crescendo in a book which had a remarkable influence' and is 'widely cited as evidence of pervasive "class bias" in English education.'[16] Brian Simon and Caroline Benn also recognised that the book illustrated how the grammar schools were acting as a solvent of class divisions by preparing 'working-class children for entry to university and the professions as new recruits to the middle class'.[17] But Musgrove went on to argue that Jackson and Marsden's conclusions were wholly belied by the evidence they provided and that the book was 'the great celebratory record of the glories of the grammar school as a working-class institution', as most of the sample they studied fitted in rather well and became successful.[18] Indeed many of them looking back wanted – like the late Lord Wilson of Rievaulx – the system that produced them preserved intact. On the whole, however, the book has been as well received by academics as by students and the public. Blackledge and Hunt describe it as a 'splendid book'.[19] Reid refers to it as a 'now almost classic study' while Galloway calls it 'One of the classic studies of educational sociology.'[20] Perhaps the book's best accolade, as Alan Sinfield wrote, was to be referred to in the late Dennis Potter's *Stand Up Nigel Barton* where the eponymous hero's appeal to his working-class background is met with 'the cocktail-party remark: "There's nothing unique about that. It's been well documented in Jackson and Marsden's book." '[21]

Although *Education and the Working Class* may be Brian Jackson's best known book, his next study, *Streaming: An Education System in Miniature*, published in 1964, was almost as influential, especially among people involved in education professionally. The main theme of the book, as Sanderson and Watts have emphasised is that pressure on the heads of junior schools to gain 11-plus success led to their streaming children from the age of seven and that such streaming produced a heavy weighting of middle-class children towards 'A' streams with poorer children predominating in 'B' and 'C' streams.[22] Even some comprehensive schools were guilty of encouraging early streaming. 'The way in which streaming was a reflection of the selective system and the way in which the large comprehensive schools were accentuating the division was most forcibly publicised by Brian Jackson. . .'.[23] Moreover Brian found, as both King and Downey acknowledge, that teachers also tended to become classified as 'A' or 'B' stream teachers.[24] Even their classrooms reflected this separation, with craft work and gerbils furnishing the 'B' rooms whereas the 'A' classroom walls tended to be full of examples of the brighter children's written work. One very important trend identified by Brian Jackson and noted by three of the many writers who make some reference to the book was the tendency for children born near the end of the school year, i.e. entering school as much as 20 per cent younger than their classmates, to do less well and gravitate to the lower streams.[25] By 1983, when streaming had become very unfashionable in junior schools, Bailey and Bridges referred to *Streaming* as 'One of the by now classical critiques of streaming' though a few years earlier, as this trend gathered pace, Creer quoted Brian Jackson when sounding a note of caution: 'Silberman wholeheartedly accepts the English infant schools as a radical revolution in public education, forgetting entirely what Brian Jackson repeatedly and rigorously documents for us – that poor and working-class children in British infant schools do no better than their ancestors now in English secondary schools. . . .'[26] Nevertheless, the swing away from streaming in the years following publication of the book was dramatic. Brian Simon has written that 'probably the rapid transition to non-streaming was . . . the most important and widespread' of the very important changes in education in the 1960s.[27]

Working Class Community, which appeared in 1968, was based as noted above on research done in the late 1950s as a pilot project for the Institute of Community Studies. Much of the original work, as Brian acknowledged, was done by Dennis Marsden. Quite why Brian finally completed it when he did is a mystery but it was published at about the time he finally left Sheila, who had also worked on the early research. Was it a valediction for that period of his life? It contains a collection of essays which concern themselves with various aspects of working-class, or rather, specifically northern working-class life. One chapter, as Dennis Marsden pointed out to me, was an early classic of sociology. It described a teenage riot in Huddersfield which was repeated the following Saturday night on a grander scale as a result of press publicity, thus anticipating by several years one of the themes of Cohen's *Images of Deviance* in which it is argued that the effect of publicity is frequently to exacerbate and even to promote further social disorder.[28]

Working Class Community, like *Education and the Working Class,* was brought out in paperback by Penguin, in March 1972, and reprinted in December of that year, but it never had the impact or influence of *Education and the Working Class.* It has been criticised for a rather mawkish sentimentality in singing the praises of brass bands and pigeon fancying as important cultural pursuits, though that is a distortion of the book's theme. Bantock is particularly critical of this aspect of Brian's work: 'B. Jackson has a similar enthusiasm for brass bands, and adds pigeon fancying.' Referring to a later piece by Brian in *New Society* he continues: 'His more recent attempt . . . is to find educational potential in such manifestations as chalking on walls, pulling a motor bike to pieces or "dolling up each other's hair. . .".'[29] Elsewhere he repeats the attack calling Brian a prejudiced witness, and again citing brass bands and pigeons as the only indigenous cultural interests of the working classes.[30] Reynolds and Sullivan also have a sly dig at Brian's fondness for these two activities while acknowledging his serious points about encouraging 'working-class values such as co-operation, friendliness and a sense of community'.[31] In a restrained and thoughtful assessment of Brian's ideas on retaining 'positive aspects of working-class culture, such as a sense of community' and 'a high degree of co-operation rather than competition . . .' in the curricula of comprehensive schools, Lawton also picks upon 'interesting traditional activities such as pigeon breeding'.[32] But Kenneth Morgan cites the book as an important contribution to the climate of social realism in the arts that flourished in the 1960s, as a reaction to the spread of middle-class Tory capitalism, to show that Britain was still a markedly unequal society.[33] Perhaps the most perceptive reference to the book is that of M.P. Bender who wrote 'Jackson highlights well a tension in many left-wing novelists, e.g. Orwell, and social scientists: the attempt to retain their identity and at the same time fuse it into a strongly knit group.'[34] For Brian Jackson was middle class, as he admitted during a question and answer session in Melbourne during his lecture tour of Australia in 1972 with Ivan Illitch.[35] He enjoyed both the cultural and the more visceral pleasures of middle-class life; books, music, wine and good food. Brian even criticised A.S. Neill, a hero of his in many respects, saying 'There are crucial decisions in education that children can't take because they don't know enough . . .' and he illustrated the point with 'Neill stops the argument with "You like pop: I like Ravel. Let's agree to differ." But Ravel is better than pop, and that's not merely a matter of opinion, but of focused, sifted opinion whose accumulation over generations represents the cultural values that education should open up to children.'[36]

Brian's comment illustrates clearly the dilemma he faced of wanting to broaden children's horizons and open their minds to centuries of rich European culture without destroying their sense of community with their warm and friendly working-class roots. It was the dilemma of his own life and it was to be manifested time and again to the very end. Was *Working Class Community* too romantic, or even just plain wrong? Is the true face of working-class culture perhaps the 'nasty, Nazi, Essex skinhead' with a home-made tattoo on his forehead and a can of lager in his hand, from whom Brian would have 'run a mile'.[37] Or can all the world's problems be solved over a cosy chat in the *Rovers Return*?

For much of his time Brian's writing consisted of technical matter relating to ACE and NEC, such as booklets and reports. His journalism too was frequently an extension of, or connected with, his major campaigns and preoccupations of the time. He had written articles in the *Guardian* – including the notorious one on 24 July 1963 recommending that Princess Anne should be sent to a comprehensive school – to publicise ACE's work from when he took it over in 1962. His first review – of 'One off: The story of an advertising man' – commissioned by Bill Webb, the paper's long-serving literary editor, appeared in December 1964.[38] He wrote regularly from then until his death, producing dozens of reviews on subjects ranging from sociology and education to literature and books for, and about, children. His last *Guardian* piece appeared on 16 June 1983.[39] During this period Brian became a friend of Bill and Shelagh Webb. In the early 1970s they were living in Manchester and Shelagh was a teacher, with four small children, who had already led a campaign to let parents into hospitals with their sick youngsters. Brian encouraged her efforts to bring parents into the school at Gorsey Bank in Stockport to run assemblies and so forth. As many others have reported, she felt Brian had a knack of making her feel that what she was doing was both worthwhile and important.[40]

Brian also produced several features in both the *Sunday Times Magazine* and, later, in the *Observer Magazine*. Godfrey Smith, then editor of the former, remembers that if they wanted anything on education they would simply call Brian, and both he and his then deputy, Peter Crookston, remember Brian as a fount of brilliant ideas.[41] For the *Sunday Times Magazine* he wrote 'A Progressive Parent's Primer' on 26 November 1967, '100 Years of State Schools' in January 1970 and, with colleagues from ACE, he produced a massive eight-week series entitled 'Parents A–Z of Education' between January and March of that year.[42] In 1971, as described in Chapter 6, the magazine sponsored an ACE scheme for schoolchildren to test for pollution in rivers around the country and the results were announced by Brian, in conjunction with Geoffrey Young who ran 'Things of Science' for ACE, in November 1971 as 'The Clean River Report'. The two collaborated again the following year on a similar scheme to test for clean air – partly by observing the spread of lichens – and the results of this were described in January 1973.[43] Articles by Brian on pre-school children, single parents, and starting school appeared in February, March and September of 1973.[44]

It was the *Observer*'s turn to publish some of Brian's educational journalism in 1974. Articles on similar themes appeared as a three-part series entitled 'Living with Children', written with Sonia Jackson and Anne Garvey, in the *Observer Magazine* during September and October. Also in October Brian collaborated with Anne Garvey on a piece about corporal punishment for the *Sunday Times Magazine*.[45] In 1978 Brian produced a three-part series for the magazine entitled 'All the world's a classroom' which dealt with the needs and rights of children from 4-7, from 7-12, and during their teens.[46] He also wrote two longish illustrated pieces for the magazine describing long-distance walks he and Sonia made on Hadrian's Wall and along the Ridge Way from Ivinghoe Beacon in Hertfordshire to Overton Hill, Wiltshire.[47]

Brian wrote various pieces for the *New Statesman*. These were mostly on serious political or educational topics. Paul Barker, for many years editor of *New Society*, felt that this was Brian's preferred platform for such writings.[48] Brian capitalised on his 1972 trip to Australia by writing a rather tongue-in-cheek 'An evening with Ivan Illitch' for it the following year.[49] 'Call me Iva-a-n' the article began, and went on to describe how the ascetic El Greco guru interrupted his spaghetti and, surrounded by pretty girls, proceeded to harangue him, and through him the world at large. Brian concluded that the great revisionist deschooler was possibly nothing more than a maverick Catholic quack: a travelling showman. Perhaps he was just upset by the impossibility of competing for female attention with an attractive priest. And yet, he wrote, despite the paradoxes of the man would we, without his sort, ever begin to ask questions at all?.[50]

Brian also wrote articles and reviews regularly, as might be expected of a sociologist, in *New Society* from 1964 until just before he died.[51] Most of the findings of his sociological researches first saw light of day in its columns and from the mid 1970s he occasionally reviewed books by other experts in his own field.[52] He also wrote occasionally for the trendy and intellectual, though sadly short-lived, women's magazine *Nova*, between 1969 and 1975. A classic example of his work there was a piece on the rights and wrongs of sex education for young children which took as its title a quote from a sex-education lesson of the late Michael Duane of Risinghill: 'You probably know them as balls.'[53] These pieces were for Peter Crookston who commissioned work again from Brian when he moved to the *Observer*.

One long-running campaign for which Brian sought wide publicity in a variety of media was for a Minister for Children. Indeed it became an obsession with him. Several people have confirmed that he wanted to be that minister, though how he expected to achieve this without serving several years as a back-bench Member of Parliament, is hard to imagine, unless he hoped, like Michael Young, to be ennobled. Bill Webb, a great admirer otherwise, said Brian could be a pain in the neck at times and that this obsession amounted to megalomania.[54] Frank Pedley, at one time Vice Chairman of ACE, felt that Brian had always had a rather grandiose idea of his own importance and Sue Owen, who worked with Brian on the TV programme for childminders, *Other People's Children*, confirmed that he was obsessional about being such a minister.[55] In an interview with the late Brian Redhead, in the last episode of this series, Brian clearly ignored the rehearsed speech and said, 'Of course, what we really need, is a Minister for Children', leaving poor Brian Redhead to pick up the pieces of the script and close the programme.[56]

Brian Jackson first proposed a Minister for Children in January 1974 when he addressed the Paediatrics Section of the Royal College of Medicine.[57] He seems to have been motivated by the tragic case of Maria Colwell who, though seen by all the professionals – policeman, social worker, doctor, teacher – nevertheless died because none of them took overall responsibility for her case and there was no co-ordination between departments. This lack of co-ordination, he said, reflected the position at government level. Pointing out that children were the only large minority group in the community without a strong political spokesman he spelled out the case for such a ministry in a long article in *New Society* in January 1976.[58] This coincided with some private lobbying Brian did when he addressed a seminar at Sunningdale called by the Department of Health and Social Security. The seminar was attended by Dr Owen as the Minister and it was allied with the department of Education and Science whose Minister, Joan Lestor also attended. Outlining the paucity of educational and social resources for the very young, Brian acknowledged the bleak economic climate and went on to make several proposals for improving matters in a cost-effective way, tying these in to his central theme of co-ordinating resources through a ministry exclusively dealing with the needs, both social and educational, of children.[59] Having tried without success to persuade both the professionals and the government, Brian sought a wider audience the following year with an article in the *Sunday Times Magazine*.[60] This posed ten questions on the theme 'When is a child not a child?' which looked at legal, social and safety aspects of childhood and adolescence, commenting that a new Minister would have to 'ring half of Whitehall to get the answers.'[61] Two years later 1979 was the International Year of the Child. Perhaps the most poignant piece Brian wrote pleading for a Minister for Children that year appeared in the *Puffin Club Magazine*. Referring to a child's right to play, he recalled that he got the *Sunday Times* to re-direct children's letters to Santa to him and one little girl wrote, 'I don't know if you can find me. I live at 101. It's got a green door. . . . Please try. I think it's difficult to find me. I'm in the sky and there's nowhere to play up here so please come.'[62] A further two years on and Brian was still campaigning for his Minister as is clearly shown by an enthusiastic letter from a delegate to the Pre-school Playgroups Association, whose annual conference he had addressed, proposing that the PPA should back his campaign by lobbying backbench committees.[63] And finally, back in the *Sunday Times Magazine* he wrote an open letter to 'Mr Speaker, sir, I would like to submit a modest proposal on behalf of some fifteen million of our fellow citizens who did not vote at the last election. . . .'. It appeared – a supremely apposite epitaph – on the morning of the day he died.[64]

Brian Jackson never abandoned his early love of literature or his connections with the *Use of English*. He was, by all accounts, a brilliant teacher himself, and could hold his own with the best as a literary critic of books for children.[65] In 1970 he reviewed four books for children by Philippa Pearce and compared the latest of these – *The Children of the House* – with the work of E Nesbit, calling it a 'classic'.[66] This elicited letters from the author, thanking Brian for sending her a draft and from the late Edward Blishen, no mean authority on children's literature himself, saying 'I simply can't imagine a better or more perceptive essay on Philippa's work. . . . Beautifully done . . . just what I wish I had said myself'.[67]

In June 1974 Brian turned briefly to books by producing an edition of Richard Jeffries' Victorian children's classic, *Bevis*, for the late Kaye Webb at Puffin, which sadly did not sell in anything like the quantities both Brian and she believed it would achieve.[68] The following year he returned to the 'campaign trail' when he published, with Anne Garvey, a booklet on the Chinese children of Britain. This developed the themes first reported in their *New Society* article of the same name and it represented the first, and for many years the only serious look at this significant, though largely invisible, minority.[69] M.J. Taylor quoted their findings repeatedly in a more detailed study over a dozen years later and, with some reservations, confirmed their largely impressionistic conclusions.[70]

In one of his many attempts to reach an audience wider than the *Guardian*-reading middle classes, Brian wrote a couple of pieces for the *News of the World* in 1971.[71] In a wide-ranging article Brian commented that Outward Bound schemes for a troublesome boy would only turn him into a commando-like criminal and said children should be given more say in the running of their schools. Silly rules about clothing should be scrapped. He quoted a remark from a fourteen-year-old girl called Harriet who 'when asked what change she would make in her school said "I would like my school to have a sense of humour".' [72] But his major breakthrough came in 1975 when Margaret Carter, then features editor for *Living* magazine, asked him if he would write on children's matters for her.[73] His first five articles 'Living with Children' appeared between June and October 1975. They were to prove the start of a long series of pieces he wrote for Margaret and, after she left to edit *Mother* magazine, for her successor. From January 1976 until November 1981 he produced an article almost every month but with the appointment of a new editor in October 1981 his contract was terminated in January 1982.[74] The letter was written by her deputy, Ann Scutcher, but added a personal invitation to lunch which he appears to have taken up as he was in contact with Scutcher, then at *Home and Law* Magazine, over an article on working mothers for which he was to receive £150, in April 1983.[75] Brian's association with Margaret Carter proved to be both friendly and lucrative. She cajoled or chivvied him as necessary over deadlines, edited several articles into a successful book, also called *Living with Children,* published in 1980 and constantly sought to boost his earnings.[76] When she moved to *Mother* she both commissioned work from him and gave him a consultancy and it was she who suggested he walk, and write up his journey, along the Ridge Way which passed by the back of her house near Tring.[77] One article he wrote for *Mother* dealt with a subject which like so many of Brian's interests is still of topical concern. It was based on studies conducted in the United States showing how little time on average fathers spent with their babies.[78]

Towards the end of the 1970s Brian returned with a vengeance at Sonia's suggestion from the rather ephemeral world of journalism to writing books. *Starting School*, a charming description of their first year at a Huddersfield primary school was a study of six children from different ethnic minority groups.[79] *Mother* magazine gave excerpts from it in a lovely colour spread and the *Guardian* also featured it.[80] Like much of Brian's sociological work it is impressionistic in style but, in so far as he sought out the children's home backgrounds before they joined the school, it is a pioneering study. Taylor and Hegarty said 'Jackson's perceptive account . . . gives stimulating insights into experiments in multiracial education and positive and frank appraisals of aspects of the hidden curriculum. . .'. To be sure, the teachers not only knew nothing of the children's home background or culture, they even persisted in asking Muslim, Hindu or Sikh children for their 'Christian' names.[81] This book sold quite nicely, too, covering its advance and paying £174 in royalties in its first year.[82]

As a result of his connection with *Living* magazine (Margaret Carter arranged the deal) Brian wrote *Your Exceptional Child*, which was a study of seven children who were different from the average.[83] Some were exceptionally talented – the child chess-prodigy Nigel Short was one of them – others were athletically or musically outstanding while one girl was autistic and another child was being educated at home.[84] The book was a 'pot boiler' written in conjunction with a Thames TV series and gained massive publicity and favourable reviews but despite this it failed to earn sufficient royalties to cover the generous £2,500 advance.[85] Even though the book was published in a Spanish edition the royalties were still over £1,000 short of the advance when Brian died.

One curious book, *The Black Flag*, which was published in 1981, deals with the case of two American anarchists, Niccolo Sacco and Bartolomo Vancetti, and seems out of place in Brian's *oeuvre*. It started out to be a book of socialist martyrs – one of Brian's favourite books was Foxe's *Book of Christian Martyrs,* possibly a reaction to his Roman Catholic background – but he became fascinated with their case.[86] As he wrote in a Prelude to the book,

> I do not know why I began to write this book. I had never before heard of Nicola Sacco and Bartolomeo Vanzetti. . . . No. My interest then and now was in martyrs. *Why* was it that some man or woman, by the moment and the manner of their dying, pulled the future towards them, twisted the skeins of the world in improbable and unexpected ways?[87]

The most important book he published during the late 1970s is undoubtedly *Childminder* but this, being the culmination of several years research, will form the basis of another chapter.[88] Finally, at the time of his death, Brian was putting the finishing touches to a book about fatherhood which was based on interviews with a group of expectant mothers and fathers before, during and after the births of their babies. The book discussed the event from a father's point of view. It was written to illustrate, one of Brian's major later themes: that children, both boys as well as girls, were not properly educated to become parents themselves, and that such education was essential for future generations who were unlikely to pick up the necessary knowledge by being part of a large extended family. In one respect it brings to a full circle Brian's sociological work which began with the benefits of such a working-class background. It was published posthumously, with a loving introduction by Sonia.

None of Brian's subsequent writing had the impact or influence of

Education and the Working Class. It is arguable that he tried to spread his talents too widely. Possibly, despite an ability to write well, his real talents lay elsewhere. His claim to have had 'an immense influence' through having 'a way with words' may seem overly immodest. But *Education and the Working Class* and *Streaming* are each surely important enough books on which to found a reputation.

Notes

1. 'I've had an immense influence – you always do if you have a way with words.' Brian Jackson quoted in 'Epitaph for a man of ideas', *The Times Educational Supplement*, 8 July 1983.
2. Pocket book kept for tax purposes, April 1980 to June 1984. SJ2.
3. Eric Midwinter, *The Times*, 5 July 1983.
4. 'Epitaph for a man of ideas', *The Times Educational Supplement*, 8 July 1983.
5. Letter to the author, 16 August 1993.
6. Press release, 'NEC: Four Years Work and the Future' 26 October 1967, F1. Article, 'Progress report on college that offers second chance' *Guardian*, 13 November 1967. F10.
7. 'A–Z of Education', *Sunday Times Magazine*, 18 January 1970.
8. John Izbicki, *Daily Telegraph*, 5 July 1983.
9. Brian Jackson, 'Primary school notes: a comment' *Use of English 9*, Summer 1958, p.p. 224-226, and 'Free writing: field work' *Use of English' 10*, Spring 1959, pp. 147-155.
10. Interview with Dennis Marsden, 21 September 1994.
11. I am indebted to Mark Kent who carried out this slog for me as an undergraduate research assistant as part of his BA course at the University of Huddersfield.
12. G.H. Bantock, *Education in an Industrial Society*, p.178.
13. F.T. Willey, *Education Today and Tomorrow*, p.57. A. Morrison and D. McIntyre, *Teachers and Teaching*, p.100.
14. R. Bell and N. Grant, *A Mythology of British Education*, p.178. J. Demaine, *Contemporary Theories in the Sociology of Education*, p.41.
15. C.H. Persell, *Education and Inequality*, p.139.
16. F. Musgrove, *School and the Social Order*, p.44.
17. B. Simon and C. Benn, *Half Way There*, p.50.
18. *ibid.*, p.107.
19. D. Blackledge and B. Hunt, *Sociological Interpretations of Education*, p.311.
20. I. Read, *The Sociology of School and Education*, p.78. D. Galloway, *Schools and Persistent Absentees*, p.153.
21. Alan Sinfield, *Postwar Britain*, p.235.
22. M. Sanderson, *Educational Opportunity*, pp. 50-51. J. Watts, *Towards an Open School*, p.28.
23. *ibid.*, p.28.
24. R. King, *Education*, p.28. M. Downey, *Interpersonal Judgements in Education*, p.69.
25. A.V. Kelley, *Handbook of Educational Ideas and Practices*, Gen. Ed. N. Entwhistle, p.796. E.B. Castle, *A Parents' Guide to Education*, pp. 133-134. W.A.L. Blyth, *English Primary Education Vol I*, p.62.
26. C. Creer in *Innovations in Education: Reformers and their Critics*, Ed. J.M. Rich,

p.22.

27. B. Simon, *Education and the Social Order 1940-1990*, p.380.
28. Interview with Dennis Marsden, 21 September 1994.
29. G.H. Bantock, 'A Question of Quality', in *Schooling in the City*, Eds. J. Raynor and E. Harris, p.157. Brian Jackson, 'How the poorest learn' *New Society*, 1 February 1973.
30. G.H. Bantock, 'Education and Equality', in *Education, Equality and Society*, Ed. B.R. Wilson, p.153.
31. D. Reynolds and M. Sullivan, 'Towards a New Socialist Sociology of Education', in *Schooling Ideology and the Curriculum*, Ed. L. Barton, p.183.
32. D. Lawton, *Education and Social Justice*, p.92.
33. Kenneth O. Morgan, *The People's Peace*, p.201.
34. M.P. Bender, *Community Psychology*, pp. 11-12.
35. Transcript of *Cold Comfort* the Melbourne speech, June 1972, B2.
36. Brian Jackson, 'Part of the System?', review of *Talking of Summerhill*, by A.S. Neill, *Guardian*, 17 March 1967.
37. As suggested by Dennis Marsden, 21 September 1994.
38. Brian Jackson, 'Cautionary Tale', *Guardian*, 4 December 1964.
39. Brian Jackson, 'Neill of Summerhill', *Guardian*, 16 June 1983.
40. Interview with Shelagh Webb, 13 June 1996.
41. Interview with Godfrey Smith, 26 April 1997, Conversation with Peter Crookston, 16 May 1997.
42. Brian Jackson and others, 'Parents A–Z of Education, *Sunday Times Magazine*, 18 and 25 January, 1, 8, 15, 22 February and 1, 8, March 1970.
43. Brian Jackson and Geoffrey Young, 'The clean air kit for children', *Sunday Times Magazine*, 18 June 1972, and 'Watching what we breathe', *Sunday Times Magazine*, 28 January 1973.
44. Brian Jackson, 'Before school: four nagging questions', 'Before school: the single parent', and 'Gently into the new term', *Sunday Times Magazine*, 18 February, 4 March and 2 September 1973.
45. Brian Jackson and Sonia Jackson, 'Living with children' and 'Smoothing the path to school' *Observer Magazine*, 22 September and 29 September 1974. Brian Jackson with Sonia Jackson and Anne Garvey, 'Teenage tripwires' *Observer Magazine*, 6 October 1974. Brian Jackson with Anne Garvey, 'This is going to hurt you more than it will hurt me', *Sunday Times Magazine*, 27 October 1974.
46. Brian Jackson with Margaret Roberts and J.M. Tanner, 'All the world's a classroom', *Observer Magazine*, 5, 12 and 19 November 1978.
47. Brian Jackson, 'Doing the Wall, warts and all', and 'In the steps of Stone Age man', *Observer Magazine*, 26 March 1978 and 23 November 1980.
48. Conversation with Paul Barker, 6 June 1997.
49. Brian Jackson, 'An Evening with Ivan Illitch', *New Statesman*, 26 October 1973.
50. *idem*.
51. Brian Jackson, 'Streamed and unstreamed schools', *New Society*, 19 November 1964; 'Betraying Apostle', *New Society*, 17 March 1983.
52. See bibliography of articles and reviews.
53. Brian Jackson, 'You probably know them as balls', *Nova*, December 1969; 'Why I keep on voting Labour', *Nova*, March 1970; 'Is your child getting a good education?', *Nova*, April 1973; 'How will the household cope?', *Nova*,

May 1975.
54. Interview with Bill Webb, 13 June 1996.
55. Interview with Frank Pedley, 11 June 1996. Interview with Sue Owen, 20 May 1996.
56. I am indebted to Sue Owen for lending me a Video Recording of this series.
57. ACE Press Release, 25 January 1974.
58. Brian Jackson, 'A minister for children?' *New Society*, 15 January 1976.
59. Brian Jackson, Transcript of speech, 'Ministerial responsibility for young children', January 1976, E15.
60. Brian Jackson, 'The Case for a Ministry of Children?', *Sunday Times Magazine*, 1 May 1977.
61. *idem.*
62. Brian Jackson, 'Me and the United Nations" *Puffin Club Magazine*' 23 August 1979.
63. Letter from Susan Munns, Hammersmith, 5 July 1981, E15.
64. Brian Jackson, 'Citizen's Bill' *Sunday Times Magazine*, 3 July 1983.
65. Interview with Rebecca Slim (*née* Abrams), 25 April 1997.
66. Brian Jackson, 'Philippa Pearce in the golden age of children's literature', *Use of English*, Vol. 21 No. 3, Spring 1970.
67. Letters from Philippa Pearce, 5 June 1969, Edward Blishen, 9 June 1969, F6.
68. Letter re royalties from 'Kaye' at Penguin 'Its maddening that such an admirable book hasn't settled down into a distinguished sales figure. . .', 11 May 1977, H18.
69. Brian Jackson and Anne Garvey, 'The Chinese Children of Britain', *New Society*, 3 October 1974, and NERDT, 1975.
70. M.J. Taylor, *Chinese Pupils in Britain*, pp. 52-53 and *passim.*
71. Brian Jackson, 'Children face the scrapheap' and 'Pupil power' *News of the World*, 4 July 1971, and 28 November 1971.
72. 'Pupil Power' *ibid.*
73. Interview with Margaret Carter, 11 August 1995.
74. Letter from Ann Scutcher, Deputy Editor, 4 January 1982, H18.
75. Letter from Ann Scutcher, *Home and Law* Magazine, 12 January 1983, H18, Letter to Ann Scutcher, 13 April 1983, E4.
76. Letters from Margaret Carter, 28 August 1975, 21 June 1976, SJ/MC, 9 June 1977, H17.
77. Contract at £35 a month for 12 months, 1 September 1980, H18. Interview with Margaret Carter, 11 August 1995.
78. Brian Jackson, 'When did you last see your father?', *Mother*, 14 September 1981.
79. Brian Jackson, *Starting School*, 1979.
80. 'Starting School', *Mother*, 10 July 1979, *Guardian*, 6 July 1979.
81. M.J. Taylor and S. Hegarty, *The Best of Both Worlds?*, pp. 496 and 485.
82. Letter from Croom Helm, June 1980, H18.
83. Interview with Sonia Jackson, 28 January 1996.
84. Brian Jackson, *Your Exceptional Child.*
85. Statements from David Higham Associates Ltd, Literary Agents, 1980-1983, H18.
86. Interview with Sonia Jackson, 16 August 1993.
87. Brian Jackson, *The Black Flag*, p.ix.
88. Brian and Sonia Jackson, *Childminder.*

Chapter 8
Endings and Beginnings

In 1973 Brian Jackson had been seeking a change from being the Director of ACE for some time, and he appears to have considered the possibility of a conventional job so long as it was prestigious enough to give him a national platform for his thoughts and writings. According to notes in one of his day books he had applied, unsuccessfully, for the position of Chief Education Officer to the Inner London Education Authority in 1971.[1] Although such a formal position might seem an unlikely choice for him he does appear to have seen it as a challenging opportunity to develop his ideas about education in a practical and highly public way. It could have provided him with the major role in education that he must have felt was his due. As he wrote in his application, 'The scope of the position is already very considerable, and no doubt can be made more so. It is unique, and in essence quite unlike the post of Chief Education Officer in other British cities. Its scale is its least formidable character, its versatility its most difficult, and its potentiality its most problematic.' It is tempting to speculate how he might have moulded the capital's, and possibly the country's educational system had he been appointed. After some general platitudes his draft continued:

> London is a kingdom. It is Britain in miniature, and should seek to be a model of Britain in the future. The London education service has the responsibility of serving the people of London. But it has the opportunity always of shaping the best future for education all over Britain.

It could have been an exciting experiment. But the ILEA decided not to take the risk. Brian was probably already considered too unconventional for such a position and his *curriculum vitae* was, to say the least, not specially appropriate.[2]

Instead Brian set up another project, the National Children's Centre, in Huddersfield, but he never seems to have intended to take day-by-day control of it himself. Possibly he saw himself with a more important metropolitan role or he may have recognised that routine management was not his *forte*. In this chapter I propose to examine the events leading up to the foundation of the National Children's Centre and Brian's move, shortly thereafter, to Bristol.

In 1973 Brian Jackson took up a one-year Simon research fellowship at Manchester University which meant moving back to the north of England. It was the end of an era. In other ways too it marked a watershed in Brian's life. He was nominally still joint director of ACE in the triumvirate with Eric Midwinter and Richard Blake but it was they, particularly Richard, who were effectively running the show.

The National Extension College was also now functioning successfully without Brian, thanks to his and Richard Blake's re-organisation of it during 1971. The college was able to leave its lodgings with ACE in Trumpington Street and return to its 'wooden hut' in 1972 as the Cambridge University Press had postponed its plans to redevelop the site.[3] Although, as noted elsewhere, Richard had declined the offer to take over the running of the college, Brian had persuaded two other key members of the ACE team to move. Conrad Halloran, the treasurer at ACE, became Executive Director and Richard Freeman, who had been running ACE's information services, became Educational Director, taking over the Executive Directorship in 1976 when Conrad Halloran returned to ACE to take charge of finances there once again. In response to research findings at the Open University which were summed up by Naomi McIntosh (Sargant) as the need, if it were to remain truly 'open', for an 'open' school to feed it, the NEC launched three new 'beginner's courses', one of which, *How to Study Effectively* by Richard Freeman, became the college's first best-seller as enrolments soared to 1,000 a year. This new direction was to prove successful. By 1974 total student enrolments reached 9,000 and the recovery from the postal strike seemed complete.[4]

Inevitably, with Brian's move to Yorkshire, change was afoot at ACE too. In June 1973 the governing council of ACE was broadened by the inclusion of several very distinguished names: Caspar Brook, 53, Director of the Family Planning Association, Brian MacArthur, 33, Editor of *The Times Higher Educational Supplement*, Tom McManners, 53, Senior Adviser, Lancashire Education Authority, Sir Neville Mott, 67, Master of Gonville and Caius College and recently retired Cavendish Professor of Physics at Cambridge, John Tomlinson, 41, Director of Education for Cheshire, John Moores, 45, of the Littlewoods organisation, and Frank Pedley, 53, Chief Education Officer for Rochdale, joined Reuben Heffer, 65, the Cambridge bookseller, Peter Laslett, 55, the distinguished historian who had helped found the BBC's Third Programme as well as being instrumental with fellow council members Brian Jackson and Michael Young in the 'Dawn University' experiment, John Vaizey, 43, Professor of Economics at Brunel and author of a string of books on the economics of education and Len White, 70, a barrister and former Borough Education Officer for Gosport who, in ACE's early days, had fielded all the readers' questions sent in to *Where?*[5] Yet, despite this glitter of support, ACE was about to go into its most difficult period.

The new council meeting later that year after the death of Dr White noted that there had been criticism of its composition: no women and most of the men too old to have school-age children.[6] In 1974 Richard Blake, despairing of ever improving the lot of the poor through education while the very basics of life – food and a roof over their heads – remained an unachievable goal for many, left ACE at the invitation of Douglas Tilbe, to run Shelter, the charity for the homeless.[7] At the same time Eric Midwinter, who had told Brian of the possibility in a letter the previous September, also left to become Head of Teachers' Centres for the Liverpool Local Education Authority.[8] As Brian wrote in *Where?*, this was a successful development from the Priority project:

> It is almost ten years since ACE began working on the idea of 'educational priority areas'. The breakthrough chance came when ACE's chairman Michael Young was appointed to the Plowden Committee and was able to navigate through the committee the recommendations which turned yet another maverick idea into government policy. Or at least, government experiment. . . . When the experiment was over, most of the people concerned moved off to write or lecture about it. . . . Eric . . . was prepared to carry on . . . as an autonomous ACE outpost.[9]

It was this outpost that the Liverpool Education Authority was then taking over. As Brian wrote, 'A perfect circle'. And a classic example of ACE successfully working itself out of a job.

Richard Blake's replacement was John Hipkin, a former teacher and researcher into curriculum and examinations with the Schools Council and recently involved with Brian Jackson in the Radio Cambridge campaign. Hipkin might well have seemed an ideal choice,[10] but in fact his tenure of the post was a short and unhappy one. As Brian wrote to Michael Young he had backed another candidate, Bruce Kemble, a journalist.[11] Michael Young had spent much of the previous few years in Africa and it was left to Frank Pedley to conduct the interviews.[12] Pedley, who thought Kemble unsuitable, not least because he was already earning far more than ACE could possibly afford to pay, got the impression that Brian had virtually told Kemble the job was his.[13] Hipkin's appointment was clearly not to Brian's liking. Brian and Barrie Knight took him to the pub afterwards and tried to persuade him that he would have to toe their line.[14] The explanation for this apparently bizarre behaviour becomes clear from the letter to Michael Young, referred to above, where Brian continued:

> I'm left in an awkward spot over those borderline projects (Watch, Ugandan Asians, Butlin's) which I've stuck on to ACE as host body. Not foreseeing the course of events at all well (and being abroad), I failed to switch their funding and identity in time. So I can neither stop them being killed off, nor re-invigorate them.[15]

But as we have seen he did manage to hive off the SSRC project from ACE. Partly because he did indeed kill off the Butlin's project, Hipkin seems to have been very unpopular with the ACE staff.[16] Beryl McAlhone, editor of *Where?* since the early months of 1966, left in July 1974 to become women's editor of the *Observer*.[17] Sandra Last, who had joined ACE as a young typist in the early 1960s and had returned there after having a baby, sensed the different atmosphere and left that same summer only to be recruited back a few weeks later to join the Butlin's team at Clacton.[18] Sensing a 'staff-council split' Brian had ceased to be a member of ACE's council by November 1974.[19] At the beginning of 1975 the staff remaining at ACE had rebelled. They called for a meeting with the governing council claiming they were unhappy about the way John Hipkin was running things, especially his plans to improve the centre's financial position by cutting back its activities drastically. In particular they objected to his axing its education shops at Butlin's camps 'even though this was one of the few ways in which the centre managed to reach beyond its usual middle-class clientele.'[20] Michael Young, Frank Pedley (deputy chairman) and three other members of the council met the staff delegation and, according to Pedley, their spokesman, the trouble was 'nothing too earth shattering'.[21] Nevertheless by the following year Hipkin had left and Eric Midwinter, who had joined the council in 1974, took over as Chairman when Michael Young took the honorary title of President.[22] Rick Rogers, who took over as editor when Beryl McAlhone left, Conrad Halloran, who returned from the NEC, and Stella Blake seem to have kept ACE going during 1976 and 1977, with Stella as acting Chief Executive, until it returned to London in January 1978 and Peter Newell, 37, a former deputy editor of *The Times Educational Supplement* and staunch campaigner against corporal punishment, was appointed editor.[23] This later management turned its back on all but the maintained sector of education in an attempt to dissacociate itself from both the previous elitist readership and the wilder schemes of Brian's era.[24] What went wrong at ACE? Was it just John Hipkin's different style or were the staff left in a vacuum without the charismatic leadership of Brian Jackson? It was when he left as financially viable as such a precarious institution ever can be according to Richard Blake, although he was probably unaware that the cost of re-instatement of Fitzwilliam House according to the terms of its lease would be a severe burden on the later management.[25] Was the axing of the Butlin's education shops taken as a personal affront by Barrie Knight who by then appears to have been very much Brian's personal aide? Certainly several more of ACE's old guard such as Julia McGawley, Anne Garvey and Barrie himself left to join Brian's Cambridge Educational Development Trust.

It was at this time that CEDT evolved into the National Educational Research and Development Trust, NERDT, and although the application to the Social Science Research Council for what became the 'Dawnwatch' research into childminding was submitted by Richard Blake it was Sonia Jackson and Julia McGawley of NERDT who were appointed research officers for the project under Brian's supervision.[26] This research consisted of going out very early in the morning in several large industrial cities around the country and noting the numbers of children being taken to childminders so that their mothers could go to work.[27] Brian's own field of research, so far as the fellowship at Manchester was concerned, was the effects of home environment on subsequent educational development of various ethnic minorities, especially Chinese families, and both Julia and Anne were involved in some of the groundwork for this. Clearly the two projects had considerable potential for overlap.

The extent of childminding, the problems surrounding illegal childminders, the inordinately high percentage of children of West Indian background who were thus cared for while their mothers worked and, last but not least, the potentially deleterious effects this could have on their subsequent educational attainment, were first recognised by Brian Jackson in the mid 1960s when he was establishing a string of playgroups in Balsall Heath 'a huge, poor, dismal, derelict and ignored stretch of Birmingham'.[28] It took, as Brian has written, 'five years of laborious, time-consuming discussion with government departments, local authorities, private trusts and foundations to raise the very modest money to take a small but systematic look at childminding.'[29]

The original plan was to look at childminding in a depressed area of Manchester since that was where Brian was based when the SSRC grant, announced in April 1973, became available later that year. Then, like a good sociologist, Brian thought about a control situation. Naturally enough, living in Elland, he and Sonia picked Huddersfield. Moreover he had to find a base for directing the operation and an old friend, Colin Robson of the Department of Behavioural Sciences at the Polytechnic in Huddersfield, offered Brian a room in his department which Brian gladly accepted in May 1973.[30]

Brian had been spending some time back in Huddersfield. In October 1971 he wrote about a meeting with Trevor Burgin, who he had met through the Butlin's education shops scheme and who recalled a frantic search to recover the honours board at Milnsbridge School when Harold Wilson returned as Prime Minister. The caretaker found it serving as a paint shelf and managed to get it re-gilded and put up again just in time for the visit.[31] The following February, Brian was there again on the occasion of his father's death. He recalled receiving the news on the telephone from his mother having only returned home from visiting his father the previous day.[32] In July 1972 he was back again with Trevor Burgin, described by Brian as the most distinguished educationalist in Huddersfield.[33] Trevor had just received the OBE for his pioneering work at Spring Grove school in teaching English to foreign, predominantly Asian and West Indian immigrant children, and reported how proud he had been to rub shoulders with 'buggers there who had *really* done something.' Trevor took him to the Albert pub to meet Jack Clayton who, as he recorded, 'agreed to pick out a group of Moldgreen families for me'.[34] This was to form the basis of his work at Manchester which he subsequently wrote up as *Starting School*. In addition, Trevor put Brian in touch with a cross-section of local teachers, social workers, parents and officials whose consensus of opinion was that, as the officials at the Town Hall claimed, childminding was not a problem, its extent was very minor, and that illegal childminding did not exist.[35] That settled it. Huddersfield was to be the control area.

The study began with a search for previous literature on the subject but Brian soon found this to be very slim. Only medical literature – educational and sociological shelves had nothing – touched on it and only one study, by Eva Gregory which looked at general child-care practices, focused specifically on the West Indian Community.[36] Thus it was that with his usual predilection for action Brian proposed 'Dawnwatch' which took place on a cold December day, one week before Christmas, in 1973. The idea, as he reported, was to 'Get up before dawn, be in a working-class area of any city . . . in Britain, see and feel it wake up.'[37] And above all look out for mothers taking babies and toddlers to minders. The watchers included Anne Garvey, Julia McGawley, Brian and Sonia Jackson, and Barrie Knight, and the reports from Manchester, the 'Back of Arsenal Football Ground', Leeds, Bradford, Huddersfield, Islington, London and Handsworth, Birmingham all told the same story. 'While more prosperous people . . . are normally snug and warm in bed an unknown number of working parents are tugging their small children through city streets to spend many hours in the care of childminders who receive no support, recognition, or training. . . .'[38]

It certainly began to look as though the official view that childminding was not widespread, not a problem, and that illegal childminding hardly existed, was very far from the truth, even in Huddersfield. What Dawnwatch demonstrated, according to Brian, was that similar results could have been obtained in any city in the UK.[39] In an interesting aside, which perhaps reflects his view of conventional sociological researchers who were often critical of his techniques, he pointed out that Dawnwatch, by making the observers 'cold, wet, uncomfortable, grumpy, dismayed at the early hour, the bad street lights, the gutter rubbish . . . ,' flew in the face of conventional social science research techniques where the aim was for the observer to 'strive for the maximum objectivity.' Yet at the same time 'By intensely involving the researchers in the place, people, relationship – not all of it comfortable – you breed fresh perception and insight which ultimately influences the whole structure that the research creates.'[40] Brian immediately set out to try to discover how widespread the practice really was, the extent of illegal minding, and how good or bad was the care they provided. He was also prompted to consider whether minding affected the children's subsequent chances in school life: was minding a key feature in the 'cycle of deprivation' and, in that event what would the minder need to become an agent of change – training, money, new laws, respect? Moreover the team immediately made a public statement about their Dawnwatch findings. They felt this was crucial to their main purpose of promoting public awareness of the problems in order to encourage efforts to improve the situation. For as Brian wrote later,

So much expensive research – often concerned with the deprived –

results in two or three years' accumulation of private knowledge, then the slow climb to publication which itself simply becomes the honey store which the next generation of students ransack to win their certification and relatively well-paid position in the world. Again and again the 'subjects' of the research are in no way changed or the better off because of it.[41]

This was a damning criticism of conventional sociology, though Brian did admit that open research was not without its pitfalls as, for example, when they made front-page news with their startling estimate that there were possibly 100,000 children left with unregistered minders, only to discover two years later that the National Union of Public Employees independently estimated that the true figure was more like 1,200,000.[42]

Perhaps the strongest statement of Brian Jackson's approach to sociological research is in his conclusion to the opening chapter of *Childminder* where he asks, *a propos* the problems of open research, 'Is it best to protect one's scholarly virginity, or to attempt public debate aimed at action with the best ideas and knowledge one has at the time? When is data ever final, research complete or knowledge secure?' And he goes on to maintain that the most important feature of open research is to provoke action whereas classical research avoids muddying the waters. It has, moreover 'a crude and overlooked intellectual strength'.[43] He writes, 'Research is based on data but the concluding analysis, thoughts or recommendations are untested words. They may seem to emerge logically but do they make sense in practice?'[44] Making public their primary research findings in order to provoke others into action, taking action themselves and monitoring its effects rather than waiting impotently for government to do something, was Brian Jackson believed, the right way.

Some people working with minders felt that Brian Jackson's sensationalisation of extreme cases of bad childminders was counterproductive.[45] This may explain his aggressive defence of his methods, particularly as despite stressing the importance of urgency in publication, *Childminder* did not appear until 1979, six years after Dawnwatch took place.

Brian's policy, however, soon bore fruit. The National Elfrida Rathbone Society had been established in 1965 to 'deal with all aspects of educational hardship'. Anne Evans, Assistant Director of the Society, proposed that Brian, who according to the *Observer*, which publicised the venture, seemed by then to 'have cornered the childminding field', should get his Childminding Research and Development Unit to help them run a short but intensive course for minders in Brixton.[46] Moreover the course was specifically aimed at illegal West Indian minders since children from this ethnic background were appearing in disproportionately large numbers in schools specialising in the education of those designated as educationally sub-normal. As the Society's Director, Reverend Ian Henderson said, the project was 'designed to prevent further generations of children from having to attend such schools.'[47]

This was then, and still is, a revolutionary idea. Yet highly paid professional women take professional help with the care of their young children for granted. Why shouldn't poorer working women, Brian argued, also enjoy the support of carers who had been professionally trained? Indeed, as Ian Henderson's remarks show, Brian believed that well-supported minders could replace nursery schools at a fraction of their cost and significantly improve a child's performance subsequently at school.

Julia McGawley agreed to move from research in Manchester to help to run the course but also to observe, and write it up. Then the plan was for the rest of Brian's team to go down six months later to visit the minders and evaluate the benefits of the course. Both Julia and Sonia had begun to establish what sorts of support minders actually wanted rather than what the team thought they should have: safety and play equipment, a travelling toy library. They did not want visits to a playgroup, which they saw as a challenge to their own competence, or other measures designed to release them from normal household chores to spend more time working with the children. Indeed many regarded messy, play-based education with outright hostility.[48] Thus difficulties were envisaged from the start. The next thing was to find a dozen or so unregistered minders willing to join the course which was to run for five weeks from 10 a.m. to 3 p.m. four days a week. Despite the fact that the minders were actually to be *paid* to attend, 'a sensible and realistic decision', as Brian noted, it proved impossible to recruit more than seven illegal ones and so three registered minders considered by social services as most likely to benefit from the course were included. Between them the ten looked after nineteen children.[49]

Despite the fact that the course was well-endowed, supported by many child-development specialists, and considered by all involved to have over-come its initial difficulties and been a great success, when the team came back after six months to evaluate the effects they came to the conclusion that there was no observable long-term benefit either to the women who had taken part or to their young charges.[50] Brian concluded that:

> If the minder is essentially being asked to make a huge cultural leap she will need two kinds of support. Firstly the support that comes from regular contact with other minders whose husbands, parents and neighbours are, like hers, unlikely to be sympathetic, and secondly the support of the 'experts' on an ongoing basis.[51]

What they needed, he argued, was to be given somewhere to meet and talk and to feel the presence of regular support systems such as a travelling toy library. He realised that any backing given to minders would need to be of a long-term nature. In order to test if this would work he decided to provide a centre where such ongoing support could be provided. The National Children's Centre was to be the result.

Notes

1. Brian Jackson, hand-written draft of application, 1971.
2. Interview with Frank Pedley (former Chief Education Officer), 11 June 1996.
3. *National Extension College*, 1990, p.11.
4. *idem.*
5. Michael Young, 'ACE has a new council', *Where?*, 83, August 1973.
6. Minutes of council meeting, 2 October 1973, F1.
7. Interview with Richard Blake, 23 September 1994.
8. Letter, Eric Midwinter to Brian Jackson, 17 September 1973, SJ1. *Where?* 91, April 1974.
9. *Where?*, 91, April 1974.
10. *Where?*, 92, May 1974.
11. Letter to Michael Young, 29 July 1974. SJ1.
12. Michael Young was Visiting Professor, Ahmadu Bello University, Nigeria in 1974, *Young at Eighty*, p.233.
13. Interview with Frank Pedley, 11 June 1996.
14. Interview with John Hipkin, 15 October 1996.
15. According to the letter Brian had been in Australia and America. Interview with Julia Rackowe (McGawley), 16 October 1996.
16. Sue Cameron, 'Uneasy peace after ACE probe', *The Times Educational Supplement*, 7 February 1975.
17. *Where?*, 24, March 1966, and Brian Jackson, 'Adieu to the editor', *Where?*, 94, July 1974.
18. Interview with Sandra Last, 22 September 1994.
19. *Where?*, 98, November 1974. Letter to Michael Young, 29 July 1974.
20. Sue Cameron, 'Uneasy peace'.
21. *idem.*
22. *Where?*, 120, September 1976.
23. *Where?* 134, January 1978.
24. Interview with Elizabeth Wallis, ACE, 3 November 1994.
25. Interview with Richard Blake, 23 September 1994. Interview with Elizabeth Wallis, ACE, 3 November 1994.
26. Press release, 18 April 1973, E 1/2
27. Jackson, Brian, and Sonia Jackson, *Childminder*, p.3.
28. *ibid.*, p.31.
29. *ibid.*, p.33.
30. Letter, Brian Jackson to Colin Robson, 21 May 1973, E9A.
31. Brian Jackson, hand-written notebook, 23 October 1971.
32. *ibid.*, 12 February 1972.
33. Jackson and Jackson, *Childminder*, p.33.
34. Brian Jackson, hand-written notebook, 20 July 1972.
35. Jackson and Jackson, *Childminder*, p.34.
36. *ibid.*, p.34.
37. *ibid.*, p.12.
38. *idem.*
39. *idem.*
40. *ibid.*, p.13.
41. *idem.*
42. *ibid.*, p.14.

43. *idem.*
44. *idem.*
45. Interview with Sue Owen, 20 May 1996.
46. Jackson and Jackson, *Childminder*, p.203. Barty Phillips, 'Child minders go back to school', *Observer,* 13 October 1974.
47. Press release – 'First ever course for unregistered childminders', 3 October 1974. E 1/2.
48. *Childminder*, pp. 204-205.
49. *ibid.,* p.206.
50. *ibid.,* p.212.
51. *ibid.,* p.216.

Chapter 9
Elland, and the National Children's Centre

It looks as though Brian never intended to move back south again when he moved to Elland but it was not to be. Within three years he would move to Bristol following Sonia's appointment at the university there. In the meantime, with the arrival of Seth, born on 23 July 1974, he completed his extended family of six children with a son born, like himself, in Yorkshire. Possibly the recent death of his father and the thought of having his widowed mother to hand as childminder was a factor in his decision to return to the North. At any rate he certainly seems to have been happy there as countless episodes in *Living* magazine testify. Yet his brief stay was very busy and fruitful. He founded the rather grandly titled National Children's Centre in Huddersfield which continues to thrive today.

The Simon research fellowship was for one year only but when Brian moved back to the North he bought Long Lea House at Elland against his lawyer's advice.[1] For him it was perfect. A short drive took him to the M62 motorway and thence to Manchester. Above all, it was only a couple of miles over the hill from his beloved Huddersfield.

The decision to found the National Children's Centre seems to have been settled, so far as Brian was concerned when the short, intensive, course for childminders that he had staged in conjunction with the Elfrida Rathbone Society proved, on monitoring its members, to have had no lasting effect. In consequence he decided to set up a more permanent vehicle for the support and training of minders. This coincided with the end of Sonia's and Julia's first year's work on childminding for the SSRC, but with Sonia now having a new baby to look after as well as two-year-old Ellen, Brian, if he was not to take control personally, needed someone else to run the new project.

Hazel Wigmore, like Brian a native of Huddersfield and in her early forties – in fact, as it turned out, they had been contemporaries at Moldgreen infants school – had recently been a mature student after a lifetime in commerce and was specialising in teaching children from overseas in Kirklees' Advisory Unit. When Brian sounded out Trevor Burgin about a person to run the new centre he was hoping to set up Hazel's name immediately came to mind.[2] She accepted the challenge – to give substance to what was still no more than an idea in Brian's head – and, when Kirklees agreed to second her for three years and John Henniker of the Wates Foundation came forward with funds to pay for Hazel and one other the idea became a reality in the first week of the new term, September 1974.

Brian sent a circular letter inviting people to a party at Long Lea on 14

September 1974 to discuss 'a major project on childminding just launched in Huddersfield' and on the seventeenth he wrote to those who had not been able to attend asking if Hazel could call on them.[3] The 'major project' was the establishment of a permanent children's centre to continue the work of research into what sort of support minders needed and/or wanted and to attempt to supply it. At that time only one per cent of registered childminders received any support from their local authorities and the remainder, together with untold numbers of unregistered minders, got no support whatever. This ongoing work would be monitored and the results made public nationally by whatever means were appropriate. The centre would also maintain a lobbying brief through the press and directly on the relevant authorities, including Central Government, to urge improved legislation for the under-5s generally with the aim of persuading the Government to appoint a Minister for Children to co-ordinate all the matters relating to children which were, and still are, spread between a number of different departments.[4] But the first priority was to find premises for the new centre.

Huddersfield Polytechnic, which was expanding rapidly at the time, had access to various premises in and around the town. Brian's experience of working with the Priority team in Liverpool had given him a keen sense that even the most overlooked parts of our old inner cities had an abundance of what he called Victorian cultural capital: schools, churches, chapels, factories, even former municipal offices frequently lay empty and unused.[5] Surely, he believed, one of them could become a childminder's centre.

They suffered some early setbacks, notably when the building offered by the education department which they were all set to move into one Monday was claimed back 'at the thirteenth hour' on the Friday, because the roof of a local nursery school had been declared unsafe.[6] Then Dr Stuart Armstrong, Deputy Director at the Polytechnic remembered the bus sheds recently vacated by Colin Robson's new department of Behavioural Sciences.[7] Despite the unpromising picture of cavernous spaces this conjured up, it transpired that as a result of reorganisation within the new Metropolitan transport system, half of the office space was redundant and was only being used by the Polytechnic now as a spill-over place during examinations. Thus it was that Longroyd Bridge – the building itself straddled the river at the west end of the town – became the first home of the National Children's Centre.

But of course there was much hard slogging to do before this empty shed became the Centre. First of all it had to be equipped. The first 'toys' were brightly coloured plastic bobbins from the local mills which the yarn, not the cloth as Brian averred – so much for his Huddersfield roots! – came wound on.[8] These became skittles, make-believe telescopes or simply objects to 'roll, blow through, pile up' or just arrange in patterns. This was the first of a series of raids on the local community to furnish a fully equipped playroom for, in Brian's words, 'we were determined not to buy them'.[9] Old people's

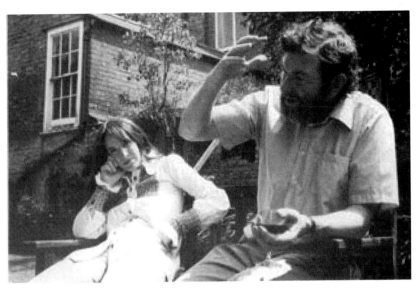

Julia McGawley with Brian in the garden at Elland

homes and the local hospital for the mentally ill, which had splendid craft workshops, were importuned to make toys. Local schools were approached on the same basis and older children's abandoned toy boxes were eagerly sought out. Thus eventually they not only had a viable playroom but also enough surplus to provide a mobile toy library to be taken in their minibus to minders' homes. All this scavenging, however, was not merely to conserve precious funds: they were making a wide network of contacts throughout the community. People were encouraged to visit the Centre and see the use to which their goods and efforts were being put. An exhibition of children's paintings gathered from local schools on the theme of living in a multi-racial society drew coach loads of school parties and these visits publicised the Centre and spread its net of useful contacts ever more widely. Let Brian take up the story in his own words.

And then we arranged a grand opening. The mayor in his gold chain, a gigantic release by children of a multi-coloured pile of balloons, lots of pictures of the children and minders on television and in the local papers. And then a continuous round of tea-and-pie lunch discussions for social workers and teachers, highly popular jumble sales, wine-and-cheese parties for childminders. It was astonishing to see the effect this had on some childminders. It was there in the sparkle of their eyes, their new hairstyle, their dress. I suspect for some – indeed I know – this was the first cheese-and-wine party they had ever attended. They loved being free of the children, being somebody, being recognised.[10]

It may be thought that the reference to cheese-and-wine parties, which displays a patronisingly yet apparently unconsciously middle-class attitude, perfectly illustrates how far Brian Jackson had come from his roots. Yet his all-pervading charm seems to have made the day. Whatever he wrote about them subsequently, he certainly knew how to make people, especially women, feel good.

Further multi-racial projects, which all promoted good public relations as well as attracting publicity to the Centre, followed. Hazel Wigmore re-arranged half the town's bus crew rotas so that the West Indian drivers' Steel band could perform at the centre.[11] Contacts through the nearby Chinese takeaway led to an evening demonstration before an audience of minders, parents, and social workers, of Kung Fu by a group of local Chinese boys. In such ways minders were brought into easy and informal contact not just with each other but with officialdom they might formerly have shunned: 'policemen, councillors, officials, social workers, health visitors.[12] Thus an air of festival and fun became a hallmark of the Centre – it still is – and played a significant part in promoting informal contacts which often produce better results than more structured meetings. It also helped enormously in raising the morale of the childminders.

But this was only a beginning. The next move was to take the work of the Centre out into the streets. In the middle of the town, where the old markets have been replaced by a modern shopping area there is an open area, surrounded by a crescent of low-level shops with names familiar on every high street, to which the developers have given the exotic title 'The Piazza'. So, one sunny Saturday morning, when most childminders were free and mothers were out shopping trailing their kids behind them, the team from the Centre set up shop with sand trays, pots of paint, climbing frames, pedal cars and a Wendy House calling the venture 'Piazza Play In'.[13] A small troupe of actors put on a children's playlet every hour and there were bold notices inviting the public to come and talk. This was the Ipswich *Education Shop* and the Butlin's experiments writ large. And it worked. Children swarmed over the tackle as soon as it came off the van. Mothers were intrigued and wanted to know what it was all about and the project team, by this time supported by a core of childminders, were busy explaining. A cameo described by Brian captures the spirit of the day:

> I recall looking for my three-year-old daughter Ellen, and glimpsing her solemnly standing at an easel painting an all blue picture, with the paint running gently downwards and dripping on the grass. And on the other side of the easel was a tramp whom one often saw picking around the market bins. He was as absorbed as Ellen, transported by the sheer strangeness of playing with brush, paper and brilliant paint. Sitting down, intently observing them were three elderly and turbaned Sikhs whose own childhoods must have been spent in the days of Kipling's Raj and endless skirmishes on the North West Frontier.[14]

'Curiously' Brian wrote, 'the right setting and the right tools brought the community into new relationships with itself – out of which action could be distilled.' He added that very formal events oddly had the same strengths. The Centre made a point of using Huddersfield's splendid 'Venetian Palazzo' of a Town Hall – a Victorian masterpiece and home of the famous Choral Society – for several events, not least to show people that it was *their* Town Hall and they had a right to use it.[15] This, according to Hazel Wigmore, was a theme dear to Brian's heart. All public buildings, such as schools, had originally been paid for in one form or another by a tax on the people. They *belonged* to the people and yet the people for the most part felt unable to enter them without a specific invitation from someone in authority. This theme goes right back to *Education and the Working Class* where so many parents were discovered to be reluctant to approach their children's schools. Brian was determined to give back to the community its communal heritage.[16]

It was in this exciting and experimental atmosphere that the Centre was launched and the public made aware of its existence. But what of its more mundane activities as a centre of action research? That was soon to follow, initiated by the redoubtable Hazel Wigmore. Looking round for under-used resources in the community, in line with Brian's ideas about enabling ordinary people and seeking the most cost-effective means to fund the project, she found that the technical college had vacancies in a crèche provided for students where courses were either free or made a nominal charge only. Why not run a course for childminders and let the children take up the spare capacity in the crèche? There were some initial problems – the course was a bit too academically slanted – but these were soon overcome and the crèche began to develop into an educationally structured playgroup while the minders especially enjoyed the 'music and movement' element which had been necessitated by a footnote which said the crèche was only for the use of students who combined physical education with their main subject. Back at the bus depot visiting 'experts' were encouraged and ranged from infant school teachers to cookery demonstrators, and even the tax inspector who explained, helpfully, that if they totted up all their expenses properly they would probably qualify for a rebate. Other sessions were devoted to group discussions where by sharing their experiences the minders became more confident as well as more knowledgeable. Within a year, at a time when hardly any training or support was available for childminders nationally, every registered childminder and several unregistered ones in Huddersfield had attended at least one course.[17]

The Centre also arranged lessons in parenthood for fourteen-year olds and above from several local schools and they too joined the crèche/playgroup and the discussion groups for their practical sessions.[18] On a similar theme of taking their action research physically into as broad a section as possible of the community they acquired a minibus. This was invaluable for bringing minders into the Centre and for taking children out to the park or sometimes the seaside, but it also enabled them to take their services out into the town. Various other under-used premises were located and, by taking the toy library to them, local groups of minders were formed. One scheme which proved particularly successful was the late Mary Crossley's idea of having them meet in health clinics where space was available for children to play and minders to meet whilst health visitors weighed babies and doctors saw adults. Thus, as Brian wrote later, everyone was 'driven more closely and usefully together' reminding him in miniature of the 'vast, unnecessary and wasteful gulf we permit between medicine and education.'[19] This was a theme which, as an element of his advocacy of a Minister to co-ordinate all matters relating to children, was constantly dear to his heart.

In such ways the Centre became involved in many communal activities over the years whose direct relevance to the under-5s may at first sight seem somewhat tenuous but which are all of a piece with Brian's grand plan for a Children's Ministry. They ran English classes for Asian mothers. They became involved with the Government's fight to eradicate adult illiteracy running one-to one tuition sessions. Many women, they found, had become minders because lack of reading skills precluded their taking work outside the home. But the consequences were disastrous. Because there were no books or papers, no stories read or scribbling pads about the house, they were passing on their problems to their charges just at the age when constructive pre-school play is so vital to future academic success. The tutors were volunteers recruited from the local community and used the existing resources of the Centre. 'Parents helping parents helping children.'[20] A key element in this diversity was the need, and the readiness, to exploit any available public funding which could even remotely be related to the welfare of children.

A spectacular, in many senses of the word, success was the 1976-77 Fundecker project. Brian had used a redundant double-decker bus as a mobile language laboratory back in the early days of ACE and Eric Midwinter had developed the idea in the Liverpool EPA project as a Playbus. Now the two functions, teaching and play, were to be combined in an ex-Bradford bus brilliantly decorated with flowers in the psychedelic style so typical of the time. The bus was initially funded by the Joseph Rowntree Charitable Trust. The conversion and painting were completed in the Centre's own workshops and the bus was launched on 5 November 1977 by Dennis Healey M.P. (later Lord Healey), then Chancellor of the Exchequer and for some time one of the Centre's trustees. It proved to be an immensely innovatory project. It was truly a community bus and it served in that capacity variously as a mobile classroom, health clinic and general meeting place for parents and childminders as well as being 'full of painting, climbing, jumping, sliding, building, drawing, singing children'.[21] It also functioned as a children's theatre, a mobile exhibition, advice, and information centre as well as touring the streets and

The Children's Centre 'Junglebus' playbus.

housing estates of Huddersfield during the summer school holidays with play schemes. Many local companies, shops and charitable organisations have helped to fund its activities over the years. The Centre subsequently adapted similar buses for other towns and, in a joint action with the BBC *Pebble Mill at One* programme, produced the first Playbus specially adapted for handicapped children.[22]

As unemployment among teenagers became an increasingly urgent problem in the late 1970s the Centre worked closely with the Government's Manpower Services Commission to operate community service schemes. The Youth Opportunities Programme aimed to provide young people in the 16-18 age group with a combination of training and work experience and the Centre welcomed the opportunity to undertake this task and broaden it by ensuring that the teams they took on were all given the option of working with children as well as doing a wide range of other socially useful work within the community. In this way some small inroads could be made in another of Brian's pet hobby-horses: Training for Parenthood.

Even more importantly the Centre adopted a policy of ensuring that the teams were all racially mixed. Brian Jackson had long worked with racial minorities such as the West Indian and Asian communities in Birmingham and had drawn attention, with Anne Garvey, to the many small isolated groups of Chinese children across the country.[23] At the time of the influx of Ugandan Asians expelled by Idi Amin he had proposed, without success, that the Government should establish a permanent Migrant Settlement Service.[24] Accordingly the Centre, situated as it is in a town with a high proportion of different ethnic minority groups, had continued to work towards encouraging the integration of people with different cultural roots: not just by learning to subsume them into English culture but by sharing them with the host community and enriching both in consequence. This aspect of action research touched the many problems facing immigrant communities: language, education, welfare problems such as loneliness and ageing and, most difficult of all, prejudice. By its work with these groups and its wide nexus of contacts with the social services, education, and other official bodies the Centre has done much to understand and help alleviate such problems. Indeed, as Brian Jackson wrote:

> Research is vital but action sees results, and results attract considerable public attention. . . . Front pages of *The Times*, full pages of the *Daily Mirror*, documentary television programmes, radio programmes, have all featured work of the National Children's Centre. Radio broadcasts in Edinburgh, Leeds, London, Nottingham, Bristol or Newcastle – at dawn or midnight – all help a little to change public opinion.[25]

One of the ways the Centre got all this press coverage and public attention was by issuing regular handouts, or 'Action Registers', as they called them. Sonia produced the first two of these in April and November 1974 while a third one was the work of Barrie Knight in May 1976.[26] And public attention attracted visitors too. All this activity generated interest from a wide area both nationally and internationally. The Central Office of Information made a film of the Centre's work and the British Council used the Centre as a placing agency for foreign visitors on Government sponsored study leave. Thirty students doing a master's degree at Melbourne University flew over to use the Centre for their practical term. There were also visits from the Chinese national basketball team from Peking, which helped to build bridges with the Hong Kong Chinese, and from the Italian delegation to International Women's Year looking for ways forward from the work of Maria Montessori.[27]

This international element was hardly surprising. Brian had lectured widely in Australia in 1972 at the invitation of the Australian Students Union, and his work in the field of education was becoming well known by this time. On his return trip he visited India and Bangladesh though as the latter was still in a state of turmoil after the recent civil war he was able to learn little of use from this part of the trip.[28] The British Council had recently sponsored him to visit New Zealand for a month during April 1974 to look at education generally and provision for younger children in particular. The most prominent result of the trip was, as already noted, Brian's letter to *New*

Society claiming, contentiously, that the New Zealanders, long thought to have tolerant, humane and enlightened policies towards their native ethnic minority, were every bit as racist and uncaring about the indigenous population as the Australians or South Africans. As Brian had a close relationship with Jenny Gunby, a New Zealander who had worked with him years before at ACE, he probably had a better insight than most English visitors. The publicity caused by the article probably did him no harm at any rate.[29]

It was while Brian was in New Zealand that Jennifer Wates contacted him.[30] The original funding for the National Children's Centre came from the Wates Foundation, and other funds, as we have seen, were either generated by the Centre or provided by various Government schemes. Wates suggested that The Save the Children Fund put up the money for the Centre to have two childminding advisors in January 1975 and, with Julia McGawley moving from Manchester to Brixton it was decided to create one new post on her former 'Dawnwatch' patch: the Trafford, Stretford and Moss Side areas of Manchester. Sue Owen, an advisor on under-fives in the social services department was appointed.[31] There was no attempt to duplicate the Huddersfield Centre in Manchester. For a start it was a much larger city and its poorer areas were much more disparate. There was not the same community with which to integrate. There were many problems too, not least the rigidly disciplinarian attitude of the West Indian church elders who were horrified at the *laissez-faire* style of drop-in centres Sue developed. Gradually these gelled into four, in Longsight, Levenshulme, Moss Side and Trafford which were staffed largely by social science students from Manchester Polytechnic on secondment for their one-term of practical experience. The minders themselves helped create a toy library and the vital minibus was provided by Bird's Custard. A trip in this to an outpatients department with an innocently acquired cut led to an administrative mix-up which resulted in a report of battering at an illegal childminders that caused a near riot and almost ruined Sue's efforts. Brian made the point later that, ironically, this sort of episode was precisely what justified their softly-softly approach in such educationally and materially impoverished areas.[32] Officialdom in general frequently proved recalcitrant. One community liaison officer invited to visit an unregistered minder to see what might be done to help refused point blank to enter saying that to do so would be to connive at a criminal act. Doubtless this would be one of the occasions when, as noted by Sue Owen elsewhere, Brian could be quite abrasive. Nevertheless the work continued and eventually one of the original minders who had been visited during 'Dawnwatch' became a member of the team as part of a job-creation scheme.

Another way in which the National Children's Centre used action to gain publicity as well as to improve conditions directly was by holding a series of conferences. The first such National Conference on Childminding was her-

alded by a fanfare of publicity in local and national newspapers including
the *Sunday Times*, Brian's old stand-by, and was held in Bradford on Saturday
19 April 1975.[33] These conferences became, in Brian's words, 'an essential
part of the National Children's Centre's policy of drawing people together,
from Whitehall and Westminster, and all over the country, to look at innovative
methods of social intervention.'[34] He went on to elaborate:

> It is vital that whatever the results of research or action unfold that
> the National Children's Centre is able to radiate them. We have built
> up a network to do just this. In Whitehall we have opened up contact
> at under-secretary level and in the relevant Ministries. . . . The Think
> Tank's Report on 'Services for Young Children with Working
> Mothers' says . . . we have not undertaken any special research
> project as part of our study . . . we have however drawn on the
> research of others.

Brian noted that the National Children's Centre had been 'pleased to be
able to help and advise. . . .' He also stressed that they felt it essential that
children should be kept in a politically neutral area and that Members of
Parliament from both houses and all shades of opinion should hear of their
work. Both Sir Keith Joseph and Denis Healey were Honorary Vice Presidents
of the Centre at the time he wrote.

One visitor to the conference was Ann Goddard. She received a bouquet
for having travelled furthest – from Taunton – to be there. It was very fitting
therefore that when, a couple of years later as a result of the television
series, *Other People's Children,* a National Childminding Association was
formed to amalgamate the various viewing groups – an idea promulgated by
the Centre – she should become the first Chairman of its National Executive.
The Association was launched, within five months of the screening of the
last programme in the series, at Birmingham Town Hall with 200 delegates
present. Patrick Jenkin MP, then Opposition spokesman on Social Affairs,
was the principal speaker and within three years the Association had grown
to represent some 4,000 members.

These conferences were largely the work of Barrie Knight who, ably
assisted by Sandra Last as secretary, maintained the Cambridge end of the
National Educational Research and Development Trust, NERDT, which was
still nominally the parent organisation of the National Children's Centre.[35]
They were responsible for some notable achievements, not least the Radio
Nottingham Amnesty which flushed out so many unregistered minders and,
with Margaret Constable taking the lead, the subsequent and seminal
'Childcare Switchboard'.[36] But there were problems too. One delegate to the
Bradford conference wrote to say that it was a 'waste of time and expense'
as the MPs and Civil Servants who were 'billed as speaking in the morning
did not materialise'. She wanted to know if this was misrepresentation or
mismanagement. Sadly it appears there may have been an element of both,

as the Cambridge end of NERDT eventually collapsed in the late 1970s with massive debts and, but for the re-launch of the National Children's Centre as an independent organisation, would have brought the Centre down with it.[37]

Perhaps the most practical manifestation of this aspect of Brian's work was his role as administrative secretary of the All-Party Parliamentary Group for the Under-Fives, which he held from its inception in 1974. This group, whose Chairman and Secretary had at different times included Christopher Price MP, Sir George Young MP, Baroness Faithfull, Joan Lestor MP, Peter Hardy M.P. and Helene Hayman M.P., hoped to co-ordinate cross Ministry provision of services for children and 'create a pre-school dialogue between both Chambers of Parliament, policy making statutory bodies, and field workers'. One example of the practical work the Group did was a report, based on a visit by Brian, Helene Hayman and Barrie Knight, to Holloway, and with Joan Lestor to other women's prisons, to investigate the conditions of babies who were in prison with their mothers.[38] The Group was doubtless intended by Brian to show the importance of communication between different Ministries with the ultimate aim of the establishment of a Minister for Children. Yet just as the cracks were beginning to show at the Cambridge end of NERDT things were not easy for Brian himself. By the mid 1970s the inflation caused by the world oil-crisis made grant money harder to find. When the Simon fellowship ended in 1974 and he had severed his links with ACE and NEC in Cambridge Brian was without a formal income. Julia McGawley had left NERDT to run another Brixton experiment and her replacement was funded, as already noted, by the Save the Children Fund but Anne Garvey was 'sacked' as she put it, in the summer of 1974 at the Malt Shovel in Elland where she had gone to have it out with Brian after an acrimonious and unsuccessful negotiation with Barrie Knight.[39] Then in November 1974 she wrote to Brian, albeit in a personally friendly vein, but complaining that she was still owed £300, being the salary for June and a month in *lieu* of notice, and not the £150 he had mentioned in a note to her.[40] She referred to a 'private' conversation with Barrie where he had said 'I'm going to tell Brian it's either you or me.' Although there seems to have been a clash of personalities involved the simple truth was probably that the Trust could not afford the salary of either of them.

Writing was a vital supplement to Brian's income at that time. Fortunately he started to produce his regular monthly pieces in *Living* magazine in June 1975 and there was an increase in the number of reviews he produced for Bill Webb at the *Guardian* from about the same time.

Brian again began to seek a job. In an attempt to stay in the North he wrote to the Rector of Huddersfield Polytechnic and, referring to a conversation 'over lunch the other day' put himself forward as his 'number two', if the position had not already been settled, as he was 'ready to resign his Cambridge positions and seek a challenging post in the North'.[41] The reply came brutally quickly however, the Governors had decided on an internal appointment for Deputy Rector, and the list for a further Assistant Rector was already closed.[42] Brian also applied for the Chair of Education at Bristol University. This was not perhaps the major national educational role he might previously have aspired to but still it would have been a prestigious position. Perhaps surprisingly, for during the heady days of expansion of higher education in the 1970s many people who had done less were getting senior posts, he was not accepted. Once more it was the end of an era. Number 19 Henleaze Gardens, in Bristol's airy suburbs, beckoned. And once again four-year-old Ellen featured prominently. As Brian later recalled in *Living*, he had got the family and loads of gear in their old VW Bus up to the M62 junction at Ainley Top when they had to return to Long Lea to retrieve Tee-Tee, her silent but indispensable companion.[43]

Why had Brian not taken control of the National Children's Centre himself? Perhaps he doubted its long-term funding capabilities, especially in view of the changed climate after the oil crisis of 1973. More likely he did not want the mundane routine involved in running the Centre. Perhaps he felt that he should try to re-make his career as a writer.

Notes

1. Interview with Peter Soar, 22 September 1994.
2. Interview with Trevor Burgin, 25 May 1994.
3. Copy letters, address list, E9A.
4. National Children's Centre, *Quinquennial Report*, p.9.
5. Brian Jackson and Sonia Jackson, *Childminder*, p.217.
6. *ibid.*, p.218.
7. Interview with Colin Robson, 27 November 1995.
8. Jackson and Jackson, *Childminder*, p.219.
9. *ibid.*, p.219.
10. *ibid.*, p.220.
11. *ibid.*, p.220.
12. *ibid.*, p.221.
13. *ibid.*, p.222.
14. *ibid.*, p.222.
15. *ibid.*, p.222.
16. Interview with Hazel Wigmore, 28 May 1993.
17. Jackson and Jackson, *Childminder*, pp. 223-224.
18. *ibid.*, p.225.
19. *ibid.*, p.225.
20. *NCC Quinquennial Report 1980*, p.22.
21. *ibid.*, p.23.
22. *NCC Progress Report 1982*, p.8.
23. 'The Chinese children of Britain', *New Society*, 3 October 1974, pp. 9-12.
24. Letter to *New Society*, 18 October 1973.
25. *NCC Quinquennial Report 1980*, p.31.
26. NERDT *Action Registers*, E19.

27. Jackson and Jackson, *Childminder*, p.226.
28. Letters to Sonia Jackson, various dates, late June 1972.
29. Letter 'Maori and Paheka' *New Society*, 30 January 1975, plus correspondence in several subsequent issues.
30. Letter from Sonia to Jennifer Wates 22 May 1974, E19.
31. *NCC Action Register No.2*. E19.
32. Jackson and Jackson, *Childminder*, p.230.
33. Report on 'First Ever National Conference on Childminding', E21.
34. *NCC Quinquennial Report 1980*, p.39.
35. Jackson and Jackson, *Childminder*, p.268.
36. Brian Jackson, *Childcare Switchboard*.
37. Officially at Brown's Hotel, Dover Street, London, 19 January 1982, E14.
38. *NCC Quinquennial Report 1980*, p.41.
39. Interview with Anne Garvey, 22 September 1994.
40. Letter from Anne Garvey, 27 November 1974, SJ4.
41. Letter, Brian Jackson to K.J. Durrands, 20 June 1974, G14.
42. Letter, T.J. Gaskell, Assistant Director, Personnel and Welfare, Huddersfield Polytechnic, to Brian Jackson, 21 June 1974, G14.
43. Brian Jackson, 'Does Moving House Unsettle Children?', *Living*, May 1977 (Tee-Tee is a scrap of cloth, still happily extant in 1974).

Chapter 10
Bristol – the Final Phase

Number 19 Henleaze Gardens, Bristol was to be Brian's final home though he made regular visits to the National Children's Centre in Huddersfield and maintained his links with Cambridge through Sandra Last who continued to type all his work at home after the closure of the NERDT office. Brian, never a stranger to travel, made several foreign trips during these last years, possibly attempting to create a new international image for himself. These were sad and rather bitty years with Brian never really finding fulfilment. During his final trip to Australia, for the International Year of the Child, 1979, he helped to launch Contact Incorporated. This was probably his last significant achievement. But Brian continued to generate income from freelance journalism and, in addition to producing articles and reviews, he got to work again on a series of books. Towards the end of the 1970s and early 1980s – *Living with Children, Your Exceptional Child* and *Starting School* all appeared. The first of these was a compilation of articles he had written for Margaret Carter when she edited *Living* magazine and she helped him put it together in one week. She has described it as 'one of the happiest weeks of my life', despite Brian 'sitting in the room drinking' and tearing up her photostats.[1] It was she, too, as already noted, who arranged for him to write the second of these titles, purely as a – very lucrative – pot-boiler, in conjunction with the TV series.[2] The third of these books was researched and written in six weeks, according to Sonia, although its theme reflects the subject of his Simon fellowship research.[3]

The Black Flag, which is totally out of context with Brian's other work, looks as though it was written in response to Sonia's suggestion that Brian should pursue his career as a serious writer and in particular that he should look to an international audience rather than just a British one. He had been working on the book for some time as is clear not least from the acknowledgement of Julia McGawley whose association with Brian ceased several years before the book was published.[4] The acknowledgement ends with the one sentence paragraph, 'My deepest debt is to Sonia Jackson.'[5] 'You always said I should grasp America and I'm sorry to confirm, you were right.' he wrote to her from Boston.[6] He stayed in Concorde with Richard and Valerie Kahan and their six children whom he described as lovely and who clearly made him feel at home: Richard, a successful lawyer who 'makes lots of money . . . which his family spends even faster. . . .Valerie quite different, delightful person locked up in children, family and horses . . .' and, he continued, 'the family is totally heathen, had to get a book about [son Joshua, who had just broken a leg skiing] being Barmitzvah'ed. Richard is screwing

Sonia Jackson with Seth.

up his courage to ring the Rabbi.'[7] Brian added that he had 'struck it off' with the Governor (Mike Dukakis) and thenceforward all doors opened for him. Brian wrote that he liked it as well as Huddersfield or Cambridge, 'it is certainly an environment I should long ago have mastered.'[8] He sounds to have begun to sense the possibility of recognition at last and to have at the same time had his eyes opened to much broader horizons. 'What a mass of contradictions' he wrote, 'these prosperous Jewish families are – most embarrassing snobbery and display all mixed up with streaks of radicalism and generosity. . .'.[9] After the book was published he returned to America in 1981 to 'plug' it and appeared on several radio and TV programmes in Boston where as an Englishman he met, as he expected, with hostility from people sympathetic to IRA 'H'-Block hunger strikers. 'Can't say I find them intimidating,' he commented, 'it all seems much more amateurish and under-resourced than in UK'.[10] Indeed, as he frequently had lectured in Northern Ireland 'as nobody else will go', and had been given a forced conducted tour of Derry by two IRA men in 1978, he was hardly likely to be put out by hostile Bostonian audiences.[11] Besides, the book had sold 1,000 copies pre-publication.[12] He appeared on one phone-in programme all about the book as 'lots of old people still remembered, and still hated, Sacco and Vancetti'.[13] Although Routledge did not promote the book in New York, Brian went there too and mentioned meeting several new people as well as looking up old friends. He spent a night with the late Bob Rapoport who 'loves his job' and 'who couldn't have been more friendly' and wrote that he walked everywhere in

New York 'just to get the sight and smell of the place' and that he felt he had strengthened his links there and now had 'the outline of a presence.'[14]

Before the collapse of the London end of NERDT Brian was still slogging away at projects as well as keeping a close eye on the development of the National Children's Centre. In April 1977, following on his work with Anne Garvey and its development by the National Children's Centre, NERDT organised the 'First Ever National Conference on the Plight of Chinese Children in Britain' at the Commonwealth Institute in London.[15] The first week in May that year saw the Radio Nottingham 'Childcare Switchboard', described in detail elsewhere, and its later siblings on other local radio stations, which NERDT not only mounted but subsequently monitored for the SSRC.

Another small source of income was lecturing. As an expert on matters relating to children he addressed a group of young civil service high flyers, no doubt glad of the opportunity not just to collect a fee but also to influence the next generation of administrators, at the Civil Service College in February 1977 on 'Children's Rights'.[16]

In the summer of 1978 the Calouste Gulbenkian Foundation and the British Council joined forces to fund a visit by Brian Jackson and Hazel Wigmore to Australia to attend a conference in Melbourne arranged by L'Organisation Mondiale pour L'Education Prescholaire (OMEP).[17] They had several meetings with Professor Ron Goldman, formerly Pro-Vice Chancellor of La Trobe University (and before that head of Didsbury Teacher Training College, Manchester), whose postgraduate students they entertained at the National Children's Centre, and carried out a busy schedule of engagements, making several contacts throughout Australia.[18] After a terrible journey out – the plane broke down in Bombay – and a general shortage of cash, Brian reported in a letter to Sonia that the media, at least, loved him if no one else did.[19] 'I only wish I was as well known at home as here,' he wrote, 'I've met several people here who have copies of *Other People's Children*.'[20] And perhaps most significantly he confessed: 'Books, books, books, you're right: it's the secret.'[21] Brian and Hazel sold many copies of this booklet and there was also a considerable interest in his report of the Childcare Switchboard Experiment. Brian was invited to address delegates from all the Australian states at a meeting convened by Mr Pat Lanigan, Director General, Department of Social Security, to discuss proposals for the coming International Year of the Child, and this report excited most interest. It was photocopied by the Government and 'distributed widely throughout Australia.'[22] As Brian commented 'seeds are well planted.'[23] Indeed they were, for the following year Brian was invited back by the New South Wales committee, funded by the DSS in Canberra, responsible for the IYC project called 'Contact'.

Brian was in Australia for three weeks, 5-30 June 1979.[24] He was met at the airport by June Jeremy, a charming and formidably efficient woman who was the project co-ordinator, and Anne Gorman, Director of the Family and

Children's Services Agency, and launched into a hectic schedule of visits, meetings and fact-finding trips accompanied by June.[25] The project was for all of New South Wales so included not just Sydney but also visits to the industrial town of Newcastle and, courtesy of the Flying Doctor Service (themselves appropriately enough pioneers of distance care since 1937), to Broken Hill and Wilcannia. This latter is an aboriginal settlement in the far West of the state, which had many social problems. Brian reported from Wagga Wagga that he still felt jet-lagged after being in Australia three days, but he seemed to relish visiting remote parts of the country; 'Nolan Australia, where most Ozzies have never been'.[26] 'Hope you don't mind the possums' said one of the locals he met, 'I expect they plague you at home too'.[27]

Throughout his stay Brian took every opportunity to publicise 'Contact'. As he reported:

> I have spoken to more than a thousand Australians personally about 'Contact'; to far more than that at public meetings, seminars and committees; and presented our case to at least a million people – may be many more – through television and radio.[28]

Moreover, he was enjoying himself enormously despite the hectic schedule and all the hard slog he was putting in. 'I'm having astonishing success with the year of the Child Project here', he wrote, 'I seem to have all the old zest plus prestige. I've set up a Childcare Switchboard here far beyond what we could afford to do in England. . .'.[29]

The highlight of his visit was the re-creation, on Radio 2UE, of the Childcare Switchboard Experiment during the week 22-29 June 1979. This was called the *2UE Care-For-Kids Careline.* Arranged by the NSW Secretariat of the IYC and Sydney's Radio 2UE, it came about 'entirely' as a result of the report Brian gave in his 1978 visit of the English experiment.[30] Fifty advisers from four government departments had been rostered by Tom Crozier and psychologist Helen Lynch to man ten telephones in a special studio at the station. Brian and Anne Gorman were on air from 9.00 p.m. to midnight on the Ian Parry-Ockenden show on the first Friday evening.[31] During the course of the following week over 1000 people phoned the Switchboard.[32]

The success of this experiment led to the establishment of a permanent switchboard in the form of Contact Incorporated. It was Brian's last major achievement and its staff recognise Brian Jackson as their true founder though links have not been maintained with the National Children's Centre since Hazel Wigmore's visit in the early 1980s.[33] By the mid 1990s Contact Inc. was still flourishing under the leadership of Co-ordinator June Jeremy. Its aim was to identify and articulate family and community needs and to 'support, refer, resource, and serve as an advocate for socially, culturally and geographically isolated children and their families.'[34] Contact Inc. received funding from National and Local Government in New South Wales and from many private and public commercial and charitable sources. Their newsletter was bringing up to date information on a range of issues and provision of services to some 9,000 recipients throughout NSW and beyond. They also published themselves a wide range of informational material; single sheets, booklets, posters and audio and video packages. They lobbied for, and acted as a catalyst between local groups and government, helping to apply for and get support for various community projects including specialist fieldworkers in Aboriginal areas.

From the late 1980s the Bernard van Leer Foundation of the Netherlands had helped to fund the Contact Children's Mobile which consisted of three fieldworkers in four-wheel drive vehicles who toured in the remote areas bringing playgroup facilities and information to isolated families and small communities. Finally, in 1993, the Commonwealth Department of Health, Housing and Local Government and Community Services decided to take over funding responsibility for this project.[35] Brian would have been delighted: yet another example of how one of his 'babies' had been recognised and adopted by the Authorities.

But back in England Brian was in some difficulty. He had not published anything for years and, much as he needed income, he also badly needed some sort of official status, or platform. He had been offered the post of Warden of Toynbee Hall which might have been very fulfilling, giving him scope to put his socialist ideals into practice, but Sonia was not prepared to uproot her children yet again, and certainly not to place them in such an educationally unpromising environment as the East End of London, at a critical stage of their education.[36]

Professor Neville Butler, head of the Department of Child Health at Bristol University, whom Brian had met socially through Sonia, came to the rescue.[37] Brian was a member of the SSRC Working Group on Research into Pre-School Education and he secured a grant of £29,977 for himself to look into the educational role of fathers in very early childhood.[38] In order to facilitate his researches he was appointed as a Research Associate. Effectively, he was an independently funded research Fellow – to Professor Butler. This was to be for a three-year period, commencing 1 May 1978.[39] The team at the department of Child Health were conducting a massive study of some 16,000 children born in the United Kingdom during one week: 5-11 April 1970. The project, entitled Child Health and Education in the Seventies (CHES), had already amassed a great deal of information of potential interest to Brian's proposed researches.[40] Brian appears to have been invited to join the team by Professor Butler partly to act as literary editor to the his team, who were anxious to publish their findings.[41] By 10 August 1978 Brian was able to report that he had spoken to Routledge and Kegan Paul who were prepared to publish the book in September 1979, in order to coincide with the International year of the Child, but that this would mean a very tight schedule: the manuscript would have to be completed by 20 December 1978.[42] Despite Brian's urging – he announced to a meeting 1 December 1978 that he had just submitted a manuscript of one of his own books so 'It could be done' – the book did not make it in time.[43] A meeting to chase the progress of the book was held 12 January 1979 but at the end of the month Brian was still noting that he had looked at chapters with Professor Butler but there was still not a uniform style.[44] Some idea of Brian's frustration is in evidence later that year in a letter from Bob Rapoport which includes the sentence 'Let us know if we can be of any further assistance in your NB salvage job.'[45] At the time Brian was writing a chapter on single-parent families in a book to be edited by Bob Rapoport and others. Interestingly his piece contains the very personal insight that though there are scores of reasons for the increase, demographically, of such families, many of them are simply a transient phenomenon and will merge into two-parent families again on the re-marriage of the parent.[46]

At the end of Brian's three-year stint he wrote up his 'Concluding CHES notes' including a piece headed 'Oz, Draft Finale' apparently in answer to a request from Dr Albert (Oz) Osborn, a member of Professor Butler's team with whom Brian had worked.[47] The book appeared after Brian's death; in his prologue Brian was barely able to conceal his view of such typically statistics-dominated work published, as he wrote about mainstream sociology in *Childminder*, when it was too late to be of any use to anyone.[48] After reminding the reader of some of the main news stories of that week back in 1970 he summed up as follows:

> Lastly there has been the dilemma of organising this vast amount of information. . . . By itself it is, of course, meaningless. . . . Naturally the best statistical techniques have been used to elicit order and significance out of these great Alps of data. However that itself must be preceded by the formulation of questions.[49]

And, having described at length what sorts of things the report had tried to do he concluded:

> Whether the authors have asked the right questions of the data, the reader will judge. All they are concerned to do in this book is to show the extent and nature of social inequality in their sample of five-year-olds and to point to some of the possible consequences of this for their progress through life. I hope, however, that our study will be more than just an interesting historical record, and that it can provide the basis for finding ways of improving the lives of future generations of children.[50]

So far as the SSRC itself was concerned, Brian does not seem to have been wholly at ease with it. He had been invited to join its Working Group on Research into Pre-School Education in 1975 and, continuing the theme of his battle with conventional social science, there is a note of the first meeting in 1980 that a report from him on 'Childminders and the BBC' was overdue. He seems to have made an effort to write up his findings but in June of that year, answering an enquiry by J.H. Smith, secretary to the Group, for more detailed information as to the design of his research, interview schedule and data, and 'in particular . . . how the interview data had been analysed and evaluated' Brian wrote back, 'I'm not convinced there is much point in gilding the lily, when one really needs to get the guts of this into the hands of people who can really use it positively: especially practitioners.'[51] Clearly he was not always meeting his deadlines, and though he obviously had a poor regard for some of his fellow members, the reason could also have been because he was drinking heavily, occasionally going missing for periods, by that time.[52]

Towards the end of his three-year attachment to the CHES group Brian started to write up his own latest research, conducted through the good offices of the hospital and his female colleague Dr Zulaika Ali, into fathers-to-be which was eventually published posthumously as *Fatherhood*. This was much more congenial work for Brian as it involved a subject dear to his heart and also lent itself to his particular brand of intimate and subjective research. To read it in the light of his known attitudes to action research is to feel his ache, on almost every page, to do much more than observe; to offer advice and the benefit of his own experiences both as a prospective and an actual father. However, despite having secured a contract for the book in 1980 and having received an advance royalty of £500 he had still not delivered the finished manuscript at the time of his death.[53] In a letter to his good friend Godfrey Smith he described his dilatoriness as follows,

> This morning I should have been writing a further chapter in my planned book on *Fathers*. But I have many strategies for avoiding creative work (I write letters, go to the lavatory, attend pointless meetings, make coffee, make calls). One of my most devious avoidance techniques is to browse in George's bookshop in Park Street, and I'm soon light years away from the university and my task there.[54]

The early 1980s were very difficult for Brian as, with no regular income after the end of the CHES work, he had to try to earn money throughout these later years as best he could. In the letter to Godfrey Smith quoted above he also refers to the postman bringing 'our impossible phone bill, and a stern letter from my publisher asking me when I am going to finish *Fathers*?'

Margaret Carter, who seems to have tried desperately to provide Brian with other sources of income, also felt that he put on a wonderful face but was, underneath, very sad.[55] Although his regular column for *Living* finished at the end of 1981 he continued to write occasional pieces in a similar vein for *Mother* where Margaret had become editor in March 1980. It was Margaret, too, who provided him with pocket money by retaining him as a consultant and arranged various foreign lecture trips for him including his first trip to East Europe.[56] She was the inspiration for his article on walking the Ridge Way which passed behind her house in Tring.[57] Eventually, however, these sources of income also dried up with Margaret's retirement from the editorship of *Mother* in May 1983.[58]

Brian wrote occasional pieces for *New Society* in the early 1980s and continued to produce book reviews regularly for Bill Webb, another staunch supporter, at the *Guardian*. In December 1981 he tentatively set up a project called 'Beehive' with an old friend from the Birmingham Playgroup days, Douglas

Tilbe, whose address gave the scheme its name, and sometime restaurateur Serge Lourie. Beehive was to be a consultancy on how to raise money for charitable causes, but it was intended that it would also generate some income for themselves. Douglas like Brian had a growing family to support. Beehive fizzled out by the following August having only earned a few hundred pounds for Brian but the cause of its demise may have been precipitated by Douglas's failing health – he died of cancer six months after Brian's death – rather than any inherent unsoundness of the scheme.[59] Then in 1982, through Douglas, there came what was to be a final opportunity for Brian to exercise his capacity for producing a fount of ideas.

The 'New Initiatives Group' was funded by 'Voluntary and Christian Service' the parent charity of 'Age Concern', and 'Help the Aged'. For four months, June – September 1982, Brian was retained to produce papers for discussion by the group which was to have its first meeting in July 1982.[60] Amongst many proposals Brian put forward was a paper entitled 'Age Resource' which noted that although the population was ageing those over sixty – or even younger retired people – should not be regarded as a group needing help but as themselves a resource. He suggested that senior people could be helped to contribute their knowledge and skill to the education system through local groups linked federally in a national body. Furthermore, he proposed that such a body might even have an international role similar to that of Voluntary Service Overseas or the Peace Corps which harnessed the energies of younger people for good and practical causes.[61] It was hardly a new idea as Brian had written a memo back in 1971 noting the numbers of older people taking NEC courses and proposing a 'School of Life' as a venture for the NEC.[62] In June of that year he wrote to Bob Rapoport of the Institute for Family and Environmental Research, another of the many groups Michael Young was connected with, who subsequently produced a paper for the NEC.[63] The Rapoports, Rhona and Bob, were to develop this theme later in a book which Brian reviewed in the *Guardian* commenting that although it was written in a stuffy – i.e. standardly sociological – way, its main theme, that ideally leisure is work, but liberated work, was correct.[64] Brian was to renew contacts with other old associates once again through this late venture. Eric Midwinter joined the New Initiatives Group as the representative of Michael Young's Centre for Policy on Ageing and it was this group that eventually was given credit for establishing the University of the Third Age, although, like Michael's biggest scheme, the Consumers' Association, the original idea may have come from abroad.[65] The concept of the early-retired using their knowledge and skills for the benefit of others was, as is apparent in Brian's paper 'Age Resource', an idea close to his heart, although his vision of it was clearly of a much more positively academic establishment than the rather cosy recreational institution that it eventually became. At the end, Canon Michael Yorke wrote thanking Brian for his 'enormous contribution in ideas' in May 1983 and the New Initiatives Group itself was wound up the following month.[66]

The Fun Run – Brian Jackson minutes before he collapsed.

The Bristol Folk House, an adult education centre in the middle of the city, was another of Brian's interests in his last months. As ever he was involved in a multitude of different causes and as chairman of this he had taken part in a national conference in 1982 which proposed setting up centres where the unemployed could meet. One of his last schemes was to propose an international meeting on unemployment at the Folk House for 1984.[67]

Brian was also involved with Professor Neville Butler's scheme to set up the International Centre for Child Studies. A memo from Brian in March 1982 seems to indicate that it was his idea: he was enclosing a proposal of an

'Idea and Feasibility of an International Centre for Child Studies, ICCS.'[68] The memo refers to a meeting Brian had with the professor and a subsequent trip to London to see Serge and Douglas so it seems this was a 'Beehive' project initially. By April 1982 ICCS was registered as a charity and had a prospectus of aims and a programme of fund-raising events for June to August starting with a launch appeal on the 17 June,[69] and already had a board of trustees and a long list of celebrities and Members of Parliament who had agreed to help.[70] One year later Professor Butler wrote to Brian to thank him for his advice and for his kind words about the Launch 'The kitty is now up to over £350,000'.[71]

Brian appears to have had no further connection with the Centre and, despite the success of this project, he was still unemployed. One of the very last positions he applied for, in May 1983, was as the Youth Training Scheme Co-ordinator at Bristol Polytechnic.[72] It was, as Sandra Last who was still typing all Brian's material said, very sad to see a man with Brian's talents and experience reduced to applying for such mundane work.[73] Brian's final visit to Cambridge was in June 1983, ten days before he died. Sandra felt he was putting his affairs in order, which, however, he certainly did not do.[74] Then on Sunday, 3 July, one of the hottest days for years, Brian collapsed and died while taking part in a 'Fun Run' in Huddersfield to raise money for his beloved National Children's Centre. What was to be his final article, once again calling for a Minister for Children, appeared in that day's edition of the *Sunday Times*.[75]

Brian's years in Bristol seem not to have been happy. Yet Neville Butler, Godfrey Smith and Hazel Wigmore all confirm Sonia's assertion that there were bright times, and testify that Brian could still be scintillating company.[76]

Notes

1. Interview with Paul Thompson, 25 April 1997.
2. Conversation with Margaret Carter, 11 August 1995.
3. Interview with Sonia Jackson, 28 January 1996.
4. Brian Jackson, *The Black Flag*, p.xiii, Interview with Julia Rackowe (McGawley) 16 October 1996.
5. *idem.*
6. Letter, Brian Jackson to Sonia Jackson, 17 January 1978.
7. *idem.*
8. *idem.*
9. Letter, Brian Jackson to Sonia Jackson, 27 January 1978.
10. Letter, Brian Jackson to Sonia Jackson, 7 October 1981.
11. Interview with Brian Jackson, Geraldine O'Brien, *Sydney Morning Herald*, 28 June 1979. B2.
12. Letter, Brian Jackson to Sonia Jackson, 7 October 1981.
13. Letter, Brian Jackson to Sonia Jackson, 8 October 1981.
14. Letter, Brian Jackson to Sonia Jackson, 17 October 1981.
15. Press release, NERDT, 22 April 1977.B3.
16. Letter, Mike Phillips to Brian Jackson, thanking him for agreeing to speak to an Administrative Trainee Course, 16 February 1977, E23.
17. Nancy Dexter, 'Australia lags in child care race', *The Age*, 1 June 1978, B2.

18. Brian Jackson and Hazel Wigmore, 'Some Aspects of Australian Education' report to the sponsors, October 1978.

19. Letter, Brian Jackson to Sonia Jackson, 24 May 1978.

20. *idem*. The book that accompanied the TV series on childminding.

21. *idem*.

22. Brian Jackson and Hazel Wigmore, 'Some Aspects of Australian Education'.

23. Letter, Brian Jackson to Sonia Jackson, 30 May 1978.

24. Brian Jackson and June Jeremy, 'A Consultative Report to the Committee for the NSW, IYC Project: Part II'. Informal Diary of Brian Jackson's 25 days in NSW.

25. Interview with June Jeremy, 17 December 1993.

26. Letter, Brian Jackson to Sonia Jackson, 11 June 1979.

27. *idem*.

28. Brian Jackson, 'A Consultative Report'.

29. Letter, Brian Jackson to Sonia Jackson, 18 June 1979.

30. June Jeremy, Informal diary of Brian Jackson's 25 days in NSW..

31. *idem*. Also taped excerpts of Australian radio interview with June and Brian.

32. Brian Jackson, 'A Consultative Report' .

33. Visit by the author and interview with June Jeremy, 17 December 1994.

34. Wendy Schiller 'Overview from the President' Contact *Annual Report 1992-1993*.

35. Contact Inc. *Annual Report 1992-1993.*

36. Interview with Sonia Jackson, 28 January 1996.

37. Interview with Neville Butler, 3 May 1996.

38. Fourth report of Working Group, September 1978, E6A.

39. Letter confirming appointment at £7,544 p.a. initially, 16 May 1978, SJl. Interview with Neville Butler, 3 May 1996.

40. Interview with 'Oz' Osbourn, 3 May 1996.

41. Memos of meetings about the proposed book 14 June 1978, and 31 July 1978, E17.

42. Memo. of meeting, 10 August 1978, E17.

43. Minutes of meeting, 1 December 1978, E17.

44. Memos., 12 January 1979 and 31 January 1979, E17.

45. Letter from Robert Rapoport, Director, Institute of Family and Environmental Research, 17 April 1979, SJ Misc.

46. Brian Jackson, 'Single-parent families', in R.N. Rapoport, M.P. Fogarty and R. Rapoport, *Families in Britain*, (Routledge & Kegan Paul, 1982).

47. Brian Jackson, hand-written notes, June 1981, E17.

48. Brian Jackson and Sonia Jackson, *Childminder*, p.13.

49. A.F. Osborn, N.R. Butler, & A.C. Morris, *The Social Life of Britain's Five-year-Olds.*

50. *ibid.*, p.XXV.

51. Agenda for meeting SSRC PSE Group, 25 March 1980, C9. Letter, Brian Jackson, 19 June 1980, H6.

52. Interview with Rebecca Slim (Abrams), 25 April 1997.

53. Contract details, David Higham/George Allen and Unwin, 7 February 1980, H18.

54. Letter to Godfrey Smith, n.d. kindly supplied during interview with Godfrey Smith, 26 April 1997.

55. Conversation with Margaret Carter, 11 August 1995.

56. From September 1980, booklet of earnings details, and, Internation Presse Familiale et Maternelle, Budapest, 16-19 May 1982, Brian Jackson Seminars, SJl.

57. Conversation with Margaret Carter, 11 August 1995.

58. Letter to Brian Jackson from Margaret Empson, Associate Editor, *Mother*, 17 February 1983, HW Misc.

59. Interview with Sonia Jackson, 28 January 1996.

60. Letter of appointment from Douglas Tilbe, 27 May 1982, C7.

61. Brian Jackson, 'Age Resource' unpublished paper, August 1982, SJ1.

62. Brian Jackson, memo to all NEC staff, 16 May 1971, F14.

63. Robert and Rhona Rapoport, 'Leisure for the over-50s', 14 January 1972, F14.

64. Brian Jackson, 'Playing with Figures' a review of Rhona and Robert Rapoport, *Leisure and Family Life Cycle*, in the *Guardian*, 28 August 1975.

65. Geoff Dench, Tony Flower and Kate Gavron, *Young at Eighty*, p241.

66. Letters to Brian, from Canon Michael Yorke, 13 May 1983, and Ken Bromfield, Development Officer, Voluntary and Christian Service, 10 June 1983, C7.

67. Brian Jackson, Draft proposal, June 1983, C9.

68. Memo Brian Jackson to Neville Butler, 22 March 1982, E17.

69. Progress report from Jenny Cobby to 'Dear Everyone', 22 April 1982, E17.

70. *idem.*

71. Letter, Neville Butler to Brian Jackson, 1 April 1983, E17.

72. Reference for Brian Jackson, Lord Young of Dartington to Eric Kinder, Clerk to the Governing Body, Bristol Polytechnic, 23 May 1983, G14.

73. Interview with Sandra Last, 22 September 1994.

74. *idem,* and, Interview with Natasha Burchardt, 25 April 1997.

75. Brian Jackson, 'A voice for the young', *Sunday Times*, 3 July 1983.

76. Interviews with Neville Butler, 3 May 1996, Godfrey Smith, 26 April 1997. and frequent conversations with Hazel Wigmore.

Chapter 11
Conclusion

'Culture has one great passion, the passion for sweetness and light.
It has one even yet greater – the passion for making them prevail.'

Matthew Arnold

One can think of names, Rhodes Boyson and A.S. Neill spring to mind, who are better known to the general public as educationalists than Brian Jackson. Brian Simon and Chelly Halsey would fill a similar role in the academic world whilst Esther Rantzen's work for children is far better recognised than anything Brian did, in England at least. Yet Brian Jackson played as significant a part in the development of education and child-welfare as any of them. In this chapter I want to assess his achievements and failures, and look at how and why they came about.

Brian Jackson seems always to have been able to get the best out of people, though perhaps he failed to get the best out of himself. 'He was' as Michael Young described him, 'an administrator who knew that the only proper purpose of administration is to release people so that they can accomplish more than they thought possible.'[1] Brian could never have launched the many schemes he did without the considerable and dedicated work of others. They do not appear to have felt they were being exploited but rather they were being given wonderful opportunities to fulfil themselves. As already noted, in Richard Blake's phrase, 'Brian *enabled* you.'

This aspect of Brian's character became apparent very early. Dennis Marsden, his contemporary at school, who, by deferring National Service was ahead of Brian at Cambridge, became a social scientist at Brian's instigation. Dennis, as he wrote in *Breakthrough*, had been miserable as an engineering student and subsequently as a supply teacher, so he jumped at Brian's suggestion that he apply to the Institute of Community Studies which had recently been set up in Bethnal Green by Michael Young.[2] It is clear from original manuscripts in Brian's archive that Dennis did much of the interviewing for *Working Class Community* as well as for *Education and the Working Class* although Brian wrote up the material for the latter and the former was eventually published under Brian's name only. Nevertheless, it was to be Dennis, not Brian, who built a successful career as an academic social scientist out of the experience.

At the other end of Brian's career, Hazel Wigmore is one of several women who received generous acknowledgement in the introductions to Brian's books, and who still looks back on the days when, as is clear not least from

Brian's own written evidence, she was moving heaven and earth to give substance to his schemes. And for a quarter of a century, in a vastly different world, she continued to run the National Children's Centre according to his inspiration and the ethos he embodied.

Perhaps Barrie Knight, who died before this work began, and who was Brian's right-hand man for a dozen years or so, epitomises the sort of loyalty Brian inspired. It was Barrie who organised many of the lectures, seminars, and conferences that Brian instigated from the days at ACE through to the late 1970s when the money ran out. Most notably he played a major role in the Butlin's education shops venture and latterly in the Radio Nottingham Childcare Switchboard. As Brian acknowledged, Barrie

> would think nothing, if the need arose, of driving 500 miles in a day
> to set up a Nottingham Amnesty or a Child Care Switchboard. Or
> just to help someone who had come unstuck in the research and
> action.[3]

Brian's 'gofer' as one colleague described him, yet according to Barrie's widow, Madelaine, he, like Richard Blake who introduced him to ACE, looked back on the years he worked with Brian as his happiest.[4]

How did Brian Jackson harness all this energy he commanded and to what purposes did he put it? What motivated him originally? What were his aims and were they worthwhile? To what extent did he succeed in achieving results?

His earliest influence was his socially deprived background of which, if he had not already sensed it, he became acutely aware of at Huddersfield College. The theme of working-class parents and children being treated as second-class citizens by the grammar school runs loud and clear through *Education and the Working Class*. His somewhat surprising decision to teach in primary schools after gaining a 'First', and his concern, later in life, with the problems of the under-privileged under-fives, seem natural in the light of this background. But it was the problems of adults who had missed out on higher education, through one reason or another, that exercised his mind when he first became an active campaigner at ACE.

His greatest achievement must be his contribution to the creation of the Open University. Although Harold Wilson and Jenny Lee gave it substance, the inspiration for it came from Brian Jackson, originally in *Education and the Working Class*.[5] As we have seen, Lord Young, describing a time when he had just taken up a teaching position in Cambridge, wrote that it was Brian Jackson who proposed that he start a new university and promised to help. Moreover having sown the seeds of the idea Brian went ahead and launched the National Extension College in 1963. This 'was established as a "prototype" for an Open University'.[6] Lord Young continued, 'At first it was just him, and no staff, but it soon began to buzz from that same tiny office as ACE's [sic]' It was there, at the NEC, that Brian demonstrated the practicality of new techniques of distance learning using new technology and coupled

Brian Jackson talking to Hazel Wigmore.

these with traditional tutorial teaching and short residential courses. These
were all techniques that the OU was subsequently to make its own. It is
possible that without this practical demonstration, and the publicity Brian
achieved for it, the government might never have proceeded with its promise
to create the OU which is now recognised as an outstandingly successful
British institution. It owes its existence, in the view of many observers, more
to Brian Jackson than to anybody.[7]

Brian Jackson is on record as saying that education is not a way to change
society but he spent a great deal of his life in trying to do just that.[8] It is,
moreover, one of the main aims of the present Labour government to do
precisely that. Furthermore the issues with which the Government is
concerned are almost entirely the same as those on which Brian fought. It is
surely timely, therefore, to look again at his work in this field.

His campaign for unstreamed comprehensive schools was one of the main
planks in this platform. Many people have said *Education and the Working
Class* had the greatest influence on the Labour Party's decision to go for
comprehensive schools. Roy Kerridge said it was the book which 'more than
any other popularised the comprehensive ideal'.[9] The Education
Correspondent of the *Daily Telegraph*, John Izbicki, credited Brian with
having 'advocated the abolition of selection and its replacement with the

comprehensive school long before Anthony Crosland sent out his notorious "Circular 10/65".[10] Like almost all the other people who argued in favour of this form of education in the 1960s and 1970s Brian was, of course, himself the very successful product of a grammar school which selected its entrants by examination and filtered them onwards and upwards towards university, and in particular the two older ones: Oxford and Cambridge. This led to a contradiction between the pursuits of excellence and of equality, which many such people, including Brian himself, recognised and struggled with.

Brian was further concerned with another dimension of contradiction. This was in the field of culture, for he recognised the worth of Shakespeare and Dickens, indeed he continued to teach English part-time at Cambridge during the 1960s, but wanted children to retain what he called their 'working-class' culture as well. What he meant by this was probably best expressed by the final 'voice' he quoted in the introduction to *Working Class Community*,

> On this estate you've got more community spirit than you would
> have, say, down Edgefield – real community. We've got to think first
> of all of getting this on a local scale; everybody in Huddersfield
> being co-operative and community-minded. Then on a national scale.
> Then on an international scale. I take it that's brotherhood.[11]

He went on to hope that 'established working-class values' would not be subsumed in the 'new world of relative affluence' to 'the poorest middle-class concerns (such as those about personal status).'[12] This feeling for the community of neighbours was classically expressed by Raymond Williams describing a lecture he attended as a young student at Cambridge where the speaker was asserting that no twentieth-century person could grasp the full significance of the word 'neighbour' in its Shakespearean sense and, interestingly enough, Leavis was 'leaning against the wall and nodding vigorously',

> Well, then I got up, straight from Pandy, so to say, and said I knew
> perfectly well what 'neighbour' in that full sense means . . . the notion
> of that kind of recognition of certain kinds of mutual responsibility.[13]

John and Lizzie Eldridge refer to this incident and write that Williams was still 'wrestling with' the statement that in a 'corrupt mechanical civilisation there are no neighbours' many years later.[14] Brian too may have continued to wrestle with this, yet faced with real working-class culture such as pop music he was horrified, as in his criticism of his friend and sometime guru, A.S. Neill, previously noted, for equating it with the work of Maurice Ravel. Alan Sinfield subjects the dichotomy to a searching scrutiny in a chapter he calls 'Left Culturism'.[15] Richard Hoggart and F.R. Leavis, both influential figures in Brian's life, are significant others who had trouble with this problem.[16] Leavis could be said to have been the major post-war influence in the tradition of Arnold of spreading the 'sweetness and light' of a 'superior' culture to the working classes, or at least to that fraction of them that had risen through the grammar schools to university. This, says Sinfield, is in keeping with Beveridge's plan that 'everyone should have the opportunity to share the good things that the upper classes had customarily enjoyed.'[17] Yet Leavis preferred the 'working-class' D. H. Lawrence – so notably defended by Hoggart at the trial of *Lady Chatterly's Lover* – to more 'effete' writers. Sinfield dismisses Hoggart's claims for working-class culture as little more than a romantic myth: 'Despite his claims for working-class culture, he makes it all sound narrow, conformist and quiescent.'

Perhaps what Brian, and many other intellectuals of the 1950s and 1960s, failed to appreciate is that for many people education is *not* perceived to be the way to greater affluence or status or even what they regard as a better quality of life. At the very time that Brian and his like were pushing for comprehensive education it was people with very different sorts of talents and abilities who were rising in society. Models such as Jean Shrimpton and Twiggy, David Bailey, the fashion photographer, pop musicians – the Beatles, who were collectively given the MBE by Prime Minister Harold Wilson, were the most famous – and, after the end of fixed maximum wages and England's World Cup success in 1966, footballers such as George Best, were all examples of this new breed of people succeeding from ordinary, or even lowly, backgrounds without the benefits of higher education.

On the other hand many people, especially the professional middle classes, continued to revere education and consider it a *sine qua non* of their continuing comfortable existence. In consequence the demand for places at public schools increased, rather than decreased, as comprehensivisation continued to spread. Moreover many of the old traditional direct-grant grammar schools when faced with the alternative of going comprehensive or becoming wholly independent, chose the latter course. Such is the demand for places that these schools, despite their high fees, continue to be able to select pupils by ability and they appear regularly in the top of the table of schools producing the best 'A'-level results. Within the State sector ambitious parents move house so as to be within the catchment area of the comprehensive schools that have higher than average academic standards, and most of these schools, while not actually using the word 'streaming', nevertheless teach many of their subjects to pupils graded according to ability, in different 'sets'.

Brian's dream of egalitarian education seemed to be well and truly dead when David Blunkett announced that Labour would not abolish the remaining grammar schools.[18] Yet in fairness to Brian, he clearly recognised and admitted latterly, that many comprehensive schools had shortcomings. According to John Izbicki, who interviewed him in 1982, he turned out to be 'almost as scathing about the 'Sixties as Rhodes Boyson.'[19] 'The trouble is that we lost contact with our constituents', Brian said, 'and they revolted'.[20] 'I must confess', he continued, 'I never saw the Black Paper riders coming over the hill and did not recognise the significance of [their] *coup d'etat'*. Brian acknowledged that Boyson and the others were right in that complete mixed-ability teaching had failed the brighter children and the comprehensives had tried to 'get everyone to fill in the valleys rather than reach the peaks.'[21]

On the question of streaming, or rather unstreaming, especially in junior schools, Brian's efforts seem to have borne more fruit. This is undoubtedly largely the result of the ending of the 11 plus examinations. However *Streaming,* whilst not a best-seller like *Education and the Working Class,* was very influential amongst educationalists and teachers. Brian Simon is surely right to imply that it played a significant part in this transformation. Moreover, as previously noted, Professor Simon feels that 'probably the rapid transition to non-streaming was . . . the most important and widespread' of the very important changes in education in the 1960s.[22]

Although Brian played an important part in influencing moves towards unstreamed schooling his efforts are now to some extent discredited. Indeed, although Brian claimed that the ability to read was the 'basis of all learning', and consequently proposed that *all* teachers should be trained to teach children to read, an unkind observer might say mixed-ability teaching deserves much of the blame for today's increased levels of illiteracy.[23] Many now agree with the late Professor Geoffrey Bantock who argued for 'disciplined learning and the authority of the teacher'.[24] Yet current policies on teacher-training reflect, yet again, how relevant Brian's ideas still are.

On a brighter note there were other successes during his time at ACE that have had an enduring benefit. A classic example of his belief in spotting a need, filling it, and then getting the relevant authority to take it on board was his universities' clearing house scheme. This scheme, which he ran in conjunction with the *Sunday Times* also illustrates splendidly another of his great gifts: the ability to publicise ACE's work through a fruitfully symbiotic relationship with the media. Less successful was Brian's scheme to create a Home and School Council. Despite a brilliant London launch and all Brian's usual backstage organisation and lobbying, the politics of the different groups involved, and their mutual distrust, coupled with their (justifiable) fear of being swamped by ACE led to the ultimate failure of this scheme. As has been shown, 'rivalry and suspicion that ACE was empire-building combined with the different interests of parents and teachers associations to wreck the idea. . . .'[25] Although it failed, many of the goals the Home and School Council had in its sights have now been achieved: parent-teacher co-operation, parent governors and the greater dissemination to parents and children of information about the school are all now commonplace.

Yet despite the triumphs there is a sense in which Brian's life was downhill from a peak somewhere in the late 1960s. He clearly expected, and with some considerable justification, to have a major influence on the Open University.

He may even have wanted to play a significant part in the running of it. But during the course of his meetings with Jenny Lee he wrote to Sonia, in Chicago at the time, of a lunch he and Peter Laslett had with the Minister at the House of Commons:

> Jennie Lee, in a vivid purple dress and beautifully dyed white-grey hair. . . . She seemed to be even more muddled in the head than before and a long way from understanding what her University of the Air ought to be like. . . . She doesn't seem to read anything or listen much, it's all anecdotes of the past or of the Cabinet and Wilson. I don't know why I like her so much, I feel she's a little fond of me and I respond, but I'm sure she pays no attention to my criticisms of the kind of university she has in mind or of the slowness of getting it started.[26]

It looks as though he blotted his copybook by being too proprietary. But maybe the Minister had already made up her mind. Certainly her ideas differed from his.

Finally, towards the end of his life, Brian did seem in Australia to be achieving the sort of recognition he craved and the opportunities it brought him to launch major schemes again – 'all the old zest' as he wrote, had come back. And he *did* achieve his final success partly in Australia. The visit in 1979 during which Brian helped to found *Contact Incorporated* came as a result of his publicising the Radio Nottingham Childcare Switchboard experiment during the previous year's visit. The idea of a permanent emergency service for children spread and was subsequently espoused in the United Kingdom by the popular TV Show presenter; Miss Esther Rantzen. This led to her establishing the service as the charity Childline in the mid 1980s.

Brian Jackson, then, was a brilliant scholar who rose from a working-class background to achieve great things. He produced not one, but at least two great ideas – the OU and a phone-in service for children – that changed British society radically in the second half of the twentieth century. His major influence on the education of children at all ages, by encouraging the abolition of the eleven-plus examination and the shift towards comprehensive schooling, was another significant achievement.

Not only did Brian produce original ideas but he had that rare quality, the ability to give them, and the ideas of others, substance. It was his enthusiasm and belief that anything that was right and desirable was also possible that motivated him. Furthermore he had the ability to carry other people along with him in a spirit of excitement. Whether they were the trustees or government officials who provided the funds or the men, and above all women, on the ground, who carried out the day-to-day work, Brian inspired them. He was a crusader *par excellence*. Yet when he died at the tragically early age of fifty he was unemployed, in debt, and almost certainly unemployable. And though he was well-enough known by those within educational circles to merit gracious obituaries in the broadsheets, he was largely unknown and unrecognised in the country at large.

Perhaps this was inevitable for Brian Jackson was a maverick. The routine life of a teacher, a writer or a journalist, at all of which professions he excelled, was not for him. But ours is a society which reveres specialisation. The day of the 'renaissance man' has long gone. Brian was generous to the point of profligacy and probably spread his talents too widely for his own good.

And what, finally, would Brian have made, had he lived, of today's world? Would he have been campaigning on an international scale, revelling in the apparently huge sums of money available for all sorts of causes in the European Community, or would he have been gloomily watching the undoing of much that he had striven to bring to pass? Was it after all better to go when, and in the way he did, running in the sun with his darling Seth at his side, to raise money for something he held dear? Was it sadly true, as one of his greatest friends and admirers said, that by then, for Brian, the glory days were over?[27]

Brian Jackson dreamt of building a New Jerusalem inspired by the words of Matthew Arnold quoted at the beginning of this chapter.[28] In his short, but brilliant, career he was more successful than most in making his dream prevail.

Notes

1. Michael Young, 'A tribute to Brian Jackson', *Where?*, No.191, September 1983, p.3.
2. Interview with Dennis Marsden, 21 September 1994.
3. Brian Jackson and Sonia Jackson, *Childminder*, p.vii.
4. Interview with Judi Thorpe, 9 January 1997. Interview with Madelaine Knight, 25 August 1995.
5. Brian Jackson and Dennis Marsden, *Education and the Working Class*, p.246.
6. *idem.*
7. Letter, Regan Scott, *Observer Review*, 22 October 1995, p.6.
8. Transcript of question and answer session after his speech 'Quality in Australian Education' at Melbourne, 26 May 1972, B2.
9. Roy Kerridge, 'A dream turned sour', *Daily Telegraph*, 11 January 1982.
10. John Izbicki, 'When bright pupils suffer' *Daily Telegraph*, 10 May 1982, p.10.
11. Brian Jackson, *Working Class Community*, p.2.
12. *ibid.*,p.3.
13. Quoted in Peter Gurney, 'Measuring the Distance', in Keith Laybourn, ed. *Social Conditions, Status and Community 1860-c.1920*, p.181.
14. John Eldridge and Lizzie Eldridge, *Raymond Williams*, p.20.
15. Alan Sinfield, *Postwar Britain*, pp. 241-245.
16. Hoggart and Williams are recommended for further reading in *Education and the Working Class*, pp. 279-280. Brian frequently attended Leavis' lectures though Tom Henn was his tutor at Cambridge. Interview with Dennis Marsden, 21

September 1994.

17. Sinfield, *Postwar Britain,* p.243.

18. 'Grammar schools will not be abolished, says Labour', *The Times,* 7 February 1997, p.3.

19. John Izbicki, 'When bright pupils suffer', *Daily Telegraph,* 10 May 1982, p.10.

20. *idem.*

21. *idem.*

22. Brian Simon, *Education and the Social Order 1940-1990,* p.380. Conversation with Brian Simon, 12 October 1996.

23. Press release, 'Children and the Election – Eight for Education', ACE, 18 February 1974, F2.

24. Obituary, Professor Geoffrey Bantock, *The Times,* 25 September 1997, p.23.

25. M. Locke, *Power and Politics in the School System,* pp. 50-51.

26. Letter, Brian Jackson to Sonia Jackson, 31 January 1967.

27. Trevor Burgin, after the funeral, as reported by Hazel Wigmore.

28. Jackson and Marsden, *Education and the Working Class,* p.243.

Epilogue
The National Children's Centre, 1983-2002

In September 2001 Hazel Wigmore, the director for twenty-seven years of the National Children's Centre, retired. Her success (described in chapter nine) in setting up the Centre originally was itself no mean achievement, but her tenacity and resolution in keeping it running after the untimely death of Brian Jackson was outstanding. Not only did she steer it through times when funding was often difficult, but she throughout kept Brian's ethos of action research and helping children and the family through example and encouragement to the forefront of the Centre's activities.

Brian's death meant the loss of a national presence for he had been regularly called on to give advice to governments on matters relating to children. This led to the Centre focussing more and more on local matters and as unemployment rose, especially among young people in the 1980s, the funds available became increasingly directed towards youth unemployment schemes. To continue to function and to complete the move into the former railway premises the Centre now occupies it was necessary to take up such schemes as were on offer, and the Centre became a major employer of building workers and care workers. Nevertheless, to keep faith with her original aims Hazel Wigmore saw to it that the youths they took on were largely those whose opportunities in the workplace were most limited by their family circumstances. Young offenders and young people from ethnic minority backgrounds formed the bulk of her recruits. She built on her long-standing connections with the Sikh and black Afro-Caribbean communities – she was seconded originally to Brian Jackson from a post as a remedial teacher specialising in helping such children – to get boys experience in the building trades and girls of hairdressing, both occupations largely closed to such minority groups at the time.

Hazel had been ably assisted in keeping the Centre running from day to day by two long-serving members of staff. Company secretary John Cashman, another former teacher who joined during Brian's lifetime, and Mike France. Mike, who has long been involved in voluntary work with Mountain Rescue, became a member of the team in September 1983. One of his many contributions has been in running a clothes and furniture exchange recycling unwanted items to families in need, and his involvement with the community service project. This is an area where the centre has combined social work with practical self-help by providing facilities for minor offenders to serve their community sentence. Using dedicated staff the resulting weekend workshops were able to restore furniture and help maintain the building. Apart from

John and Mike, most of the people associated with the Centre over the years have, of their very nature, worked on a temporary basis on various schemes or assignments, and for these the Centre frequently functioned as a training ground. Several people who worked for a short time under its aegis subsequently went on to greater things in the fields of social work and healthcare.

The shift towards more local involvement brought some benefits in that other like-minded organisations use the Centre, often as a neutral and more informal meeting ground where ideas and perhaps differences can be aired and frequently brought to a satisfactory solution. Informal contacts between such groups can be useful to both parties. Some have made a permanent home, taking up office space surplus to the Centre's own requirements and their rent has helped towards its running costs.

Hazel Wigmore, though not taking as prominent a part as Brian Jackson in public affairs, nevertheless played a national role as Director of the Centre. She joined the Voluntary Organisations Liason Committee for the Under Fives, VOLCUF, now known as the National Early Years Network, when it was first set up by the late Bridget Plowden. When Lady Plowden's succesor, Geoff Poulton, of Southampton University, was unable to continue as its chairperson Hazel took over, and having completed his term of office continued in her own right, serving in all a total of some ten years. This committee brought together the leading children's charities with some smaller organisations. During her time there Hazel chaired several national conferences and seminars. Perhaps most significantly the committee, in consultation with the chief officer of the Deparment of Health, helped to draft the Children Act of 1989.

In addition to her work at a national level Hazel Wigmore has maintained the Centre's role as a cradle of innovation throughout the 1990s. SUPAR is an acronym coined by Hazel from the two words support and parent. The idea came initially, she said, from a government initiative – which was subsequently dropped – to support families where having disabled parents sometimes meant the children were disadvantaged.[1] The intention was to use the similarity of the sound to super as a psychological boost to the confidence of parents of disadvantaged children in general. A pilot project on a local council estate was funded through a successful bid to the Department of Health. The initial approach to the proposed SUPAR mums was made by inviting them to accompany their children on the Playbus. Having built up their confidence, the women were invited to attend a day centre in a house made available by the council. Here they were encouraged to express their needs and to take steps – initially by cooking for each other – to address them. This subsequently led to several of them passing certificated courses in food hygene and first aid at work, basic skills which made them employable. In addition, of course, it added to their parenting abilities. The SUPAR umbrella has subsequently been applied by the Centre to schemes for dads and for hyperactive children. The idea has already had some dissemination and is to be written up and publicised more widely.

Another area in which the centre has continued in its role as a catalyst is in the training of nurses and social workers. The local university, the University of Huddersfield now houses the West Yorkshire School of Health and, through contacts with undergraduates over the years, Hazel realised that people from different but associated disciplines tended to view children each from his or her own professional point of view. The resulting idea of a basic common foundation course led to the creation of a unique consortium; the Nationwide Children's Research Centre, embracing the different disciplines with co-operation at executive level from the University, the Local Authority, the Health Authority, the National Society for the Prevention of Cruelty to Children and the National Children's Centre as equal partners..

One scheme which Hazel recently fostered and which has already been incorporated into national policy by David Blunkett was the 'One Stop Shop' initiative. Through her contact with the manager of Kirklees and Calderdale Employment Service she initiated a training scheme for youngsters from the Job Centre which eventually led to the payment of unemployment benefit at the National Children's Centre, thus ensuring a 'captive audience' for the training sessions. This was quite a feather in the cap of the National Children's Centre as it represented a considerable gamble by the Employment Service. The training consisted of ten half-day sessions over a period of weeks. Mr Blunkett was sufficiently impressed by the initial results to propose that similar training was written into the New Deal Gateway Programme for 18 to 24 year-olds as an intensive ten-day course.

Reference was made above to Hazel's contacts with other professional officers and this was recognized and enhanced by her participation on and graduation from a Common Purpose Initiatives group. She not only developed her skills and made further useful contacts but was nominated as one of five national winners of the New Alchemists award stemming from the concept of changing base 'metal' into gold as described in Charles Handy's book *The New Alchemists*. This award was earned for her work at the Centre including such schemes as turning a disused railway carriage and siding into a day nursery for pre-school children: the 'Playtrain, what else?'

Although as I have claimed throughout this book, Brian Jackson was the real begetter of several significant national organisations it is probably true to say that had he lived, none would have given him greater satisfaction in its work and subsequent development than his National Children's Centre: a centre of excellence devoted to his enduring passion to help the underpriviledged young.

Notes

1. Conversation with Hazel Wigmore, Tuesday, 27 November 2001

Appendix

The purpose of ACE and its journal *Where?* is to give dispassionate advice to parents about the complex educational problems their children face. Our experience is that far too little accurate information is available to pupils, parents and teachers who are constantly forming attitudes or taking decisions which may affect their lives for decades to come. We observe too, from our ordinary work, that there are several subjects, sometimes critical to young people, where frank and informed discussion is still lacking at school and home. Among these are the structure of society, and the place of the education system in it; the use of drugs (including alcohol where a recent *Where?* report estimated that 660 out of each 10,000 drinkers misuse it, and prescribed barbiturates where the estimate of misuse is 1,200 out of each 100,000), and some aspects of sex education (particularly contraception).

There are many serious matters limiting our childrens' education – more needs to be spent on education, and especially children growing up in educational priority areas. The professional standards and conditions of teachers need considerable improvement. Education needs to become more democratic, with more participation of the community, of teachers, parents and pupils at all points. We need provision for pre-school years to give all children a good start during their most formative years. The curriculum needs to equip children to deal with the actual world in which they live – a world whose violence, double standards and huge extremes of wealth and poverty they can see on their television screens each night.

Pornography is not one of these major problems facing children and parents. It is quite peripheral, and the current excitement about it distracts attention from more obvious and influential shortcomings.

The Centre has now studied the *Little Red Schoolbook,* and also sent it to a random group of 12 ACE parents, asking them whether they would let them [sic] read it.

The results of this parents jury are published in next week's issue of *Where?*, but pre-released today.

In our view few children are likely to read the book, or to want to read it. It is likely to appeal most to able and original children trying to make up their own minds. The discussion of streaming, marks, homework, school buildings, and participation offer a stimulating argument from which children will gain much. There are occasional lapses into foolishness or flippancy, but no more than in many books. The section on sex education is weakened by its decision not to discuss human feelings. But the only consistent charge which could be levelled against the book is that it polarises the views of young and old – encouraging young readers to believe in a hostile generation gap.[1]

Unfortunately the only result of suppressing the book will be to confirm this feeling. Copies will circulate even more widely among children, and will be given a glamour they previously lacked.

In our view, no good parent has anything to fear from his child reading the book, but we would advise that they discuss it together afterwards. Of the twelve ACE members who studied the uncensored version, eleven would let their children read it, and one would not. All qualified their answers, according to the age of their children and home circumstances.

Notes

1. This view appears to have been first aired by Professor John Vaizey in a friendly, hand-written, note thanking him for sending the verdicts of the ACE members, several of whom had taken up this point. (21 July 1971. G14.) It was subsequently picked up and echoed in an article in the *Times Educational Supplement*, 10 September 1971, by Philip Venning, who commented that, as ACE said, suppressing it would only exacerbate this problem.

Bibliography

Brian Jackson's Published Books and Booklets

Jackson, Brian and Dennis Marsden, *Education and the Working Class*, Routledge & Kegan Paul, 1962; Revised Edition, Pelican, 1966

Jackson, Brian, *Good English Prose, Books I and II*, Chatto & Windus, 1963

Jackson, Brian, *Streaming*, Routledge & Kegan Paul, 1964

Jackson, Brian, *Working Class Community*, Routledge & Kegan Paul, 1968; Penguin, 1972

Jackson, Brian, *1960-1970 A Progress Report*, A.C.E.,1970

Jackson, Brian, *100,000 Questions*, A.C.E., 1970

Jackson, Brian, *1,000 Children*, A.C.E., 1971

Jackson, Brian, *What did Lord Butler say in 1944?* A.C.E., 29 November 1971

Jackson, Brian, *Cambridge United*, A.C.E., 1971

Jackson, Brian, ed., *Bevis*, Richard Jefferies, 1848-1887, Puffin Books, 1974

Jackson, Brian *Starting School*, Croom Helm, 1979

Jackson, Brian, and Sonia Jackson, *Childminder*, Routledge & Kegan Paul, 1979, Penguin, 1981

Jackson, Brian, *Living with Children*, Sphere, 1980

Jackson, Brian, *Your Exceptional Child*, Fontana, 1980
    Cada Nino un Exception Ediciones Morata, 1982, Madrid

Jackson, Brian, *Child Care Switchboard*, National Children's Centre, 1982

Jackson, Brian, *Fatherhood*, George Allen & Unwin, 1983

General Bibliography

Abrams, Rebecca, *When Parents Die*, Charles Letts & Co. Ltd, 1992

Amis, Kingsley, *Lucky Jim*, Victor Gollancz, 1954

Bailey, C., and D. Bridges, *Mixed Ability Grouping*, Allen and Unwin, 1983

Banks,D., and D. Finlayson, *Success and Failure in the Secondary School*, Methuen, 1983

Banks, Olive, *The Sociology of Education*, Batsford, 1968

Bantock, G.H. *Education in an Industrial Society*, Faber and Faber, 1963

Barton, L., et.al. *Schooling, Ideology, and the Curriculum*, Falmer Press, Sussex,1980

Basset, G.W. *Innovation in Primary Education*, John Wiley and Sons, 1970

Bell, R., G. Fowler & K. Little, eds. *Education in Great Britain and Ireland*, Routledge & Kegan Paul / The Open University Press, 1973

Bell, R., and N. Grant, *A Mythology of British Education*, Panther, St. Albans, 1974

Bender, M.P, *Community Psychology*, Methuen, 1976

Benn, Caroline and Brian Simon, *Half Way There*, McGraw Hill, 1970, revised edition, Penguin, 1972

Blackledge, D., and B. Hunt, *Sociological Interpretations of Education*, Croom Helm, 1985

Blyth, W.A.L, *English Primary Education Vol 1*, Routledge & Kegan Paul, 1965

Bowker, G., *Education of Coloured Immigrants*, Longmans, 1969

Bruner, J., *Under Five in Britain*, Grant McIntyre, 1980

Burgess, Tyrrell, *A Guide to English Schools*, Penguin, 1964

Burgin, Trevor, and Patricia Edson, *Spring Grove*, Oxford University Press, Oxford, 1967

Butcher, H.J., *Human Intelligence*, Methuen, 1968

Castle, E.B, *A Parents' Guide to Education*, Penguin, 1968

Clarke, John, Chas Critcher and Richard Johnson, eds. *Working-Class Culture*, Hutchinson, 1979

Cluderay, T.M., ed., *Aspects of Education 3*, University of Hull, Institute of Education, Hull, 1965

Cluderay, T.M., ed., *Aspects of Education 15*, University of Hull, Institute of Education, 1972

Cohen, Stanley, *Images of Deviance*, Penguin, 1971

Craft, M., ed., *Family, Class, and Education: A Reader*, Longman, 1970

Croall, J., *Neill of Summerhill*, Routledge & Kegan Paul, 1983

Crosland, Susan, *Tony Crosland*, Cape, 1982

Davies, H., *Culture and the Grammar School*, Routledge & Kegan Paul, 1965

Davis, R., *The Grammar School*, Penguin, 1967

Demaine, J., *Contemporary Theories in the Sociology of Education*, Macmillan, 1981

Dench, Geoff, Tony Flower and Kate Gavron, eds. *Young at Eighty*, Carcanet 1995

Andrew Dorn, *Listening to Parents - A history of the Advisory Centre for Education*, ACE, 2000.

Downey, M., *Interpersonal Judgements in Education*, Harper and Row, 1977

Eldridge, John and Lizzie Eldridge, *Raymond Williams*, Routledge, 1994

Entwhistle, N., ed., *Handbook of Educational Ideas and Practices*, Routledge & Kegan Paul, 1990

Eyken, Willem van der, *The Pre-School Years*, Penguin, 1967

Eyken, Willem van der, *Education, The Child and Society*, Penguin 1973

Ford, J., *Social Class and the Comprehensive School*, Routledge & Kegan Paul, 1969

Feldman, G., and M. Gartenberg, eds. *Protest*, Panther, 1960

Fowler, F.D, *Language and Education*, Longman, 1974

Furlong, V.J, *The Deviant Pupil*, The Open University, Milton Keynes, 1985

Galloway, D., *The Schools and Persistent Absentees*, Pergamon, Oxford, 1985

Gittus, E., *Flats, Families and the Under-Five*, Routledge & Kegan Paul, 1976

Goldman, Ronald, ed., *Breakthrough*, Routledge & Kegan Paul, 1968

Good, T.L., and J.E. Brophy, *Looking in Classrooms*, Harper and Row, 1973

Gourvish, Terry and Alan O'Day, eds. *Britain Since 1945*, Macmillan, 1991

Green, L., *Parents and Teachers*, Allen and Unwin, 1968

Greenslade, R., *Goodbye to the Working Class*, Marion Boyars, 1976

Hall, P., et. al. *Changes, Choice and Conflict in Social Policy*, Heinemann, 1976

Halsey, A.H., ed., *Educational Priority*, H.M.S.O., 1972

Halsey, A.H., *Origins and Destinations*, Clarendon, Oxford, 1980

Halsey, A.H., *No Discouragement*, Macmillan, 1996

Hammersley, M., and P. Woods, eds. *The Process of Schooling*, Routledge & Kegan Paul / The Open University Press, 1976

Hargreaves, D.H., *Interpersonal Relations and Education*, Routledge & Kegan Paul, 1972

Hargreaves, D.H., *Social Relations in a Secondary School*, Routledge & Kegan Paul, 1973

Hemmings, R., *Fifty Years of Freedom*, Allen and Unwin, 1972

Hoggart, Richard, *The Uses of Literacy*, Chatto and Windus, 1958

Holly, D., *Society, Schools and Humanity*, MacGibbon and Key, 1971

Howe, M., *Learning in Infants and Children*, Macmillan, 1975

Husen, T., *The Learning Society*, Methuen, 1974

Illich, Ivan, *Deschooling Society*, Penguin, 1973

Izbicki, John, *Education A-Z*, Collins, 1978

Jeffcoate, R., *Ethnic Minorities and Education*, Harper and Row, 1984

Judge, H., *A Generation of Schooling*, Oxford University Press, Oxford, 1984

Kay, W., *Moral Education*, Allen and Unwin, 1975

Kazamias, A.M., *Politics, Society and Secondary Education in England*, University of Pennsylvania Press, Philadelphia, 1966

Kelsall, K., et.al. *Stratification*, Longman, 1974

Kelsall, K. and H., *Social Disadvantage and Educational Opportunity*, Holt, Rinehart and Winston, 1971

Kendall, Paul, Murray, *The Art of Biography*, George Allen & Unwin, 1965

King, R., *Values and Involvement in a Grammar School*, Routledge & Kegan Paul, 1969

King, R., *Education*, Longman, 1969

King, R., *School and College*, Routledge & Kegan Paul, 1976

Kogan, Maurice. *The Politics of Education*, Penguin 1971

Lawton, D., *Education and Social Justice*, Sage, 1977

Laybourn, Keith, ed., *Social Conditions, Status and Community 1860-c.1920*, Sutton Publishing, 1997

Littlejohn, J., *Social Stratification*, Allen and Unwin, 1972

Locke, M., *Power and Politics in the School System*, Routledge & Kegan Paul, 1974

Lovett, T., *Adult Education, Community Development and the Working Class*, Department of Education, University of Nottingham, 1982

Lovett, T., *Adult Education and Community Action*, Croom Helm, 1983

McDonald, L., *Social Class and Delinquency*, Faber and Faber, 1969

McGeeney, Patrick, *Parents are welcome*, Longmans, 1969

Macbeath, J.E.C., ed., *A Question of Schooling*, ??????????????

March, Lindsey, *The Education Shop*, A.C.E., 1966

Marshall, Gordon, *In Praise of Sociology*, Unwin Hyman, 1990

Marwick, Arthur, *British Society Since 1945*, Penguin, 1982

Marwick, Arthur, *Culture in Britain since 1945*, Basil Blackwell, 1991

Marwick, Arthur, *The Nature of History*, Macmillan Student Editions, 1973

Mays, J.B., *The School in its Social Setting*, Longman, 1967

Mays, J.B., ed., *Juvenile Delinquency, The Family and the Social Group*, Longman, 1972

Midwinter, Eric, *Priority Education*, Penguin, 1972

Miller, C.W., *Educational Opportunity and the Home*, Longman, 1971

Milson, F., *An Introduction to Community Work*, Routledge & Kegan Paul, 1974

Morgan, Kenneth O., *The People's Peace*, O.U.P., 1992

Morrison, A., and D. McIntyre, *Teachers and Teaching*, Penguin, 1969

Morrison, A., and D. McIntyre, *Schools and Socialization*, Penguin, 1971

Mortimore, J., and T. Blackstone, *Disadvantage and Education*, Heinemann, 1982

Morrish, I., *Education Since 1800*, Allen and Unwin, 1970

Mulhearn, Francis, *The Moment of 'Scrutiny'*, Verso, 1981

Musgrave, P.W., *The Sociology of Education*, Methuen, 1965

Musgrove, F., *School and the Social Order*, John Wiley and Sons, Chichester, 1979

Myers, A.R. *English Historical Documents, Vol IV, 1327-1485*, Eyre & Spottiswoode, 1969

Newson, J. & E., *Four Years Old in an Urban Community*, Allen and Unwin, 1968

O'Connor, Maureen, *A Parents' Guide to Education*, Fontana / Collins, 1986

Osborn, A.F., et. al. *The Social Life of Britain's Five-Year-Olds*, Routledge & Kegan Paul, 1984

Persell, C.H., *Education and Inequality*, New York, The Free Press, 1977

Pickard, P.M., *The Activity of Children*, Longman, 1965

Pimlott, Ben, *Frustrate Their Knavish Tricks*, Harper Collins, 1994

Pinsent, A., *The Principles of Teaching Method*, Harrap and Co., 1969

Poulton, G.A., and T. James, *Pre-School Learning in the Community*, Routledge & Kegan Paul, 1975

Rapoport, R.N., et.al. *Families in Britain*, Routledge & Kegan Paul, 1982

Raynor, J., and E. Harris, eds. *Schooling in the City*, Ward Lock Educational / The Open University Press, 1977

Ree, H., *Educator Extraordinary*, Longman, 1973

Reedy, S., and M. Woodhead, eds. *Family, Work and Education*, Hodder and Stoughton / The Open University Press, 1980

Reid, I., *Sociological Perspectives on School of Education*, Open Books, Shepton Mallet, 1978

Reid, I, *The Sociology of School and Education*, Fontana, 1986

Reisman, D., *Crosland's Future*, Macmillan 1997

Rennie, J., E. A. Lunzer and W.T. Williams, *Social Education:an Experiment in Four Secondary Schools*. Evans / Methuen Educational, 1974

Rennie, John, *Family Education: Support for the Changing Family*, Community Education Development Centre, 1986

Rich, J.M, et. al. *Innovations in Education: Reformers and their Critics*, Allyn and Bacon, 1978

Richardson, C.J., *Contemporary Social Mobility*, F.Pinter, 1977

Richardson, Linda Deer, *The National Extension College*, NEC 1990

Roberts, K, et. al. *The Fragmentary Class Structure*, Heinemann, 1977

Sanderson, Michael, *Educational Opportunity*, Faber and Faber, 1987

Sharrock, A., *Home / School Relations*, Macmillan, 1970

Shinman, S.M., *A Chance for Every Child?*, Tavistock, 1981

Simon, Brian, *Education & the Labour Movement 1870-1920*, Lawrence & Wishart, 1974

Simon, Brian, *Does Education Matter?*, Lawrence & Wishart, 1985

Simon, Brian, *Education and the Social Order 1940-1990*, Lawrence & Wishart, 1991

Simon, Brian, *What Future For Education?*, Lawrence & Wishart, 1992

Simon, Brian, *The State and Educational Change*, Lawrence & Wishart, 1994

Sinfield, Alan, *Postwar Britain*, Basil Blackwell, 1989

Taylor, M.J., *Caught Between*, NFER-Nelson, Windsor, 1981

Taylor, M.J., *Chinese Pupils in Britain*, NFER-Nelson, Windsor, 1987

Taylor, M.J., and S. Hegarty, *The Best of Both Worlds. . . ?*, NFER-Nelson, Windsor, 1985

Thompson, Paul, *The Voice of the Past*, Oxford University Press, 1978

Tomlinson, S., *Home and School in Multi-Cultural Britain*, Batsford, 1984

Ward, C., *The Child in the City*, The Architectural Press Ltd.,1978

Watts, J., *Towards an Open School*, Longman, 1980

Westergaard, J., and H. Resler, *Class in a Capitalist Society*, Penguin, 1975

Willey, F.T., *Education Today and Tomorrow*, Michael Joseph, 1964

Wilson, B.R., ed., *Education, Equality and Society*, Allen and Unwin, 1975

Wiseman, S., *Education and Environment*, Manchester University Press, 1964

Wood, M.E., *Children: The Development of Personality and Behaviour*, Harrap, 1973

Worsley, P., et.al. *Introducing Sociology*, Penguin, 1970

Yates, A., ed., *Grouping in Education*, The UNESCO Institute for Education, Hamburg, 1966

Young, Michael, *The Rise of the Meritocracy*, Thames & Hudson, 1958

Index